Root Around Britain

Root Around Britain

Henry Root's Guide to Englishness

MANDARIN

The illustrations in this book were reproduced by kind permission of the following. It is understood that those to whom acknowledgements are given are the copyright holders of the material referred to and that there can be no further reproduction without their permission:

Bath City Council page 27; The British Tourist Authority pages 28, 30, 32, 54, 72, 78, 88, 92, 143, 147 (bottom) and 154; Camera Press Ltd pages 35, 49, 57, 60, 62 (right), 99, 104, 117 and 139; Hulton Deutsch Collection Ltd pages 13, 17, 18, 30 (top), 34, 44 (top), 47, 62 (left), 64, 86 (left), 107, 127, 136 and 147 (top); Hulton Deutsch/Syndication International Ltd page 51; Mander & Mitchenson Theatre Collection page 44 (bottom); The National Portrait Gallery pages 40, 42, 53, 83, 125; Shakespeare Centre Library/Joe Cocks Studio page 84; Syndication International Ltd pages 86 (right) and 133; and Rex Features pages 16 (left and right) and 94.

The publisher has taken all possible care to trace and acknowledge the copyright holders of all the illustrations used in this book. We apologise for any errors or omissions which may have occurred; they will be corrected in subsequent editions provided notification is sent to the publisher.

A Mandarin Humour Paperback
ROOT AROUND BRITAIN

First published in Great Britain 1993
by Methuen London
This edition published in 1994
by Mandarin Paperbacks
an imprint of Reed Consumer Books Ltd
Michelin House, 81 Fulham Road, London SW3 6RB
and Auckland, Melbourne, Singapore and Toronto

Copyright © 1993 by William Donaldson
The author has asserted his moral rights

A CIP catalogue record for this book
is available at the British Library
ISBN 0 749 31692 6

Typeset by Falcon Graphic Art Ltd.
Wallington, Surrey
Printed in Great Britain
BPCC Hazell Books Ltd
Member of BPCC Ltd

Introduction

You'll have seen my chart-topping five-parter, *Root Into Europe*, featuring myself. After it, I was a pricked balloon.

'You're an *artiste* with one in the can,' my friend, Sir Attenborough, said.

Not an experience he'd have had, but I let that pass. Back in Esher, in semi-retirement now, I did what you'd do. Got up. Dressed appropriately. Into the breakfast-lounge. 'Pass the chutney, Mrs Root.' Perused the *Telegraph*. 'Old Bill Deedes. He'll have seen it all before.' Went for a stroll. 'Morning Entwistle. Funny sort of day. Neither one thing nor the other.' Came home. Measured the lawn.

It might suit you. Thirty years in middle management, then a younger man takes your parking space. Time on your hands. The woman hoovering. Her friends quacking in the kitchen. An attempt to compensate by means of an extension to the roof. DIY, is it?

It didn't suit me. Thirty years in wet fish, thereafter a communicator, a mover and shaker – you'll forgive the parlance – recently accustomed to having my head in frame. In a nutshell, I'd had a taste of media exposure, and I'd taken to it like a duck to water. Off on location with *mise en scène* and grip. 'Move over, madam. Can't you see we're filming?'

I was kicking my heels one day in Esher, when Mrs Root suggested that I involve myself in something local. She got a burst.

'*Local*, Mrs Root? I'm not local. I'm accustomed to moving on a national, if not an international, stage.'

The woman wouldn't let go, suggested that I attend the local fête. She got another burst. 'A *fête*, Mrs Root? That's women's work. Damson jam on sale in a tent? Ducking for apples with the vicar? My friend Lord Archer's books remaindered on a table?'

I attended anyway, discovered that its theme was 'Merrie England – Whither?', further that Lord Tebbit of Chingford was down to make a speech. I took charge. Called six false starts to the over-80s three-legged race. By mistake, awarded the bank manager first prize in the village idiot contest. We had to laugh. There wasn't a village idiot contest. Then I buttonholed Lord Chingford, gave him the thumbs-up *re* his speech.

'Well done, Chingford,' I said. 'Bit of a comedown, though. One minute it's all going well – a ministry car provided, up on your hind legs in the mother of Parliaments, being called a polecat by your betters – the next you're grateful to be judging a sack race in the suburbs. Never mind. Your speech – "Merrie England – Whither?" – has given me a concept.'

I could see I'd delighted him, even though his grim visage maintained an undertaker's mien. 'Root,' he said. 'You've made my day.'

I hurried home, expatiated for the benefit of Mrs Root.

'I've done Europe, Mrs Root,' I said. 'The little Greek, the bouncing Basque. This time I'll do a tour of England, seek to discover what is essentially English, whether the necessary qualities, once identified, will survive the best efforts of that ass in Brussels.'

'Sir Brittan, Henry?'

'And him, Mrs Root. I'll come in at an angle in my Euro-hat, see ourselves as others see us. As if Columbus had come the other way. Hengist and Horsa, was it? The Vikings and the other ones?'

I'd need backing, of course, but this would be forthcoming from Central Television. I'd bomb up the M1 to Birmingham, address myself to the lass in the vestibule. 'A word, if you please, with the fat man in Finance.'

This time, I'd take charge, cut out the dead wood I'd been lumbered with before, not least the chap in charge of *mise en scène*. I'd do *mise en scène* myself. Child's play. Point the camera. Cut. Pan. Fade. The sudden zoom. A fool could do it, indeed he did.

'In the first place, we'll not be filming, Mrs Root,' I said, 'merely seeking likely mugs and suitable locales. I'll need a researcher, though. Young legs to run around. We'll take the boy.'

'Henry Junior?' said Mrs Root. 'Oh – that *will* be nice!'

She got a burst. 'Not *that* boy, for goodness sake! The boy on *Root Into Europe*. Partridge, was it?'

'But you didn't care for him at all, Henry. You said he was left of centre.'

'He served his purpose, Mrs Root. And his liberal principles, so called, seldom survived a telling shot or cash in hand. A healthy *per diem*, that's the thing. I never met a *Guardian* reader who wasn't susceptible to the *per diem* – or the chance of a BAFTA nomination. Jonathan Ross on a podium. Myself in cummerbund and pumps. The Princess Royal in a dinner frock. The boy would be there, mark my words, up and down like a jack-in-the-box with his hand held out.'

Plus there'd be residuals, as before, not least an illustrated pop-up book – the responsibility for same to be in the hands of Methuen. They'd performed adequately with *Root Into Europe*, and it was only fair to give them another chance with this one.

That settled, I convened a meeting consisting of myself presiding, young Partridge and Mrs Root. I took the floor, paced the lounge-room, spoke from the shoulder on what it is to be English. Decency, justice and a sense of humour. *Sang-froid* under pressure. I mentioned the forties and the Blitz.

'There was a fellowship in the air-raid shelter, young Partridge, which the doodlebug could never know. Where did you get those trousers, by the way? Not from Peter Jones, I'll wager.'

I quoted Shakespeare, mentioned bulldog breeds and greyhounds in the slips, cited Sir Walter Hammond and Bluff Prince Hal.

'As English as Aberdeen Angus, young Partridge. The Tudor calf, the toe turned out. The gavotte, was it? The conch and minstrel? Wrestled upside down by Francis I on Flanders Field, but we'll let that pass.'

What, then, I asked, *is* an Englishman? Can one become English? What of Sir Worsthorne, the little Dutchman, or Sir Ustinov? What of Prince Philip, the moody Greek, or Sir Peter de la Billière, whose desert evolutions confounded the little Iraqi despot? What, come to that, of Sir Stormin' Norman, or the little one with legs?

'Bernard Levin, Henry?' said Mrs Root.

'That's the one, Mrs Root. It is not generally known that English is Bernard Levin's first language.'

And what of Moira Shearer, the ethnic newsreader, to say nothing of our little Asian friends? I'd interview ethnic mayors and black Tory candidates in suits, seek to discover whether our cheery Caribbean friends are settling in and picking up our ways.

As was to be expected, young Partridge gave me an argument on this, accusing me of condescension – if not worse – and suggesting that our proper provenance was the whole of Britain, not just England. What, he said, of the Scots and Welsh?

'A primitive and neurotic lot,' I said. 'Stuffed once too often by the English, do you see? Flodden, was it? Bannockburn? Robert the Bruce kebabed by a southern yeoman's spear? Owen Glendower unhorsed at Naseby? On Burns Night, the keening Scot sinks into his past, informs chance visitors such as ourselves that "the best laid plans of mice and men gang aft agley."

'And watch out in Wales, young Partridge. The Welsh traditionally pour hot cheese over things and call them rabbits. Apt in your case, but it wouldn't do much for your award-winning haircut. And I'll tell you something further: the Welsh are as superstitious as the Scots. On the night of 16th June 1992, two Englishmen were sacrificed in Cardiff High Street to Zog, the corn god. We'll not want that in Esher.'

That settled, I planned an agenda, consulted a map, drafted an itinerary which would take us from Land's End to John o' Gaunt.

'We'll do it by boat,' I said. 'The English like a boat. Raban, was it? Up the Amazon, a word with the Indians, then home again – only to be stopped in Duty Free. Or was that the Aitken woman? Either way, we'll hop ashore in Cornwall, confront a simple fisherman, busy with his nets. "What does it mean to be English, John? Speak up. You're on camera." We'll not understand a word he says. On second thoughts, we'll go by road. Pitch up at night as guests of my friend Sir Trust House Forte.'

To my surprise, Mrs Root started to demur. 'That's not very adventurous,' she said. 'Shouldn't we, like the Canterbury pilgrims of yesteryear, camp at night at whatever rude abode we stumble on?'

'I have your reference, Mrs Root,' I said. '*The Merry Wives of Bath*, was it? The very parfit gentle knight and the other one? Well, I'll tell you this. Had my friend Sir Forte been trading then they'd not have settled for a rude abode; the very parfit gentle knight wouldn't have bunked down with his horse, he'd have availed himself of Sir Forte's *en suite* fax facilities and Euro-diner.'

We were getting somewhere now. Next I identified certain traditions, institutions and characteristics which have stood the test of time. We'd examine the health of these, seek to discover, by quizzing the custodians of English values – wardens, corporals, privy seals – whether they were under threat from Brussels.

We'd dine with the Guards in barracks. At the sound of Last Post, Sloane hair stands on end, I'm told, fresh-faced young subalterns experience a softening in the loins and they quiver like defecating greyhounds.

'After the ceremony, young Partridge, parade majors clean their subalterns with a long pull-through threaded through their intestines. Military tradition, nothing more. Goats and monkeys! The boy's fainted!'

In further research of our institutions, we'd attend the State

Opening of Parliament. Lord Hailsham carried on in a fireman's lift by a Gentleman of the Chamber. Tipsy bishops snoozing on one another's shoulders. Black Rod in tights.

'Sir Horrocks, was it? A bridge too far? 2 Para picked off like plovers as they ballooned above Arnhem in the sky? In the war, young Partridge, we were fighting for freedom, so we did as we were told. Where is the boy?'

'I think he's still recovering,' said Mrs Root, 'from the visit to the Guards in barracks.'

I was getting my doubts about the boy, but I pressed on with my dissertation.

'A sense of hierarchy,' I said. 'That's the thing which separates us from the volatile Latin and tumultuous Gaul. "Take but degree away, untune that string . . ." I'm talking about class here. A dead fish rots at its head. I know fish. And so did old Bill Shakespeare. It's a pyramid – or it should be, in a well ordered society. The monarchy at the top. Under Her Majesty, the rich man in his castle. The meat in the middle, the landed or well-housed squire. At the bottom of the heap, the apple-cheeked peasant dancing round a maypole. Each man knowing his place.'

'We'll be the bourgeoisie,' said Mrs Root.

'Speak for yourself,' I said. 'Privilege, deference and an unfixed income – that's what made us great. As my friend Sir Worsthorne had it: "Patrician guilt is the enemy of Merrie England." Right – we'll be off now.'

And so we were. Into the Jaguar, the boy at the wheel, Mrs Root in the back with pork pies and Thermos flask, myself on the bridge, as it were, equipped with reporter's pad, Hasselblad and strobe. I travelled as usual with an open mind, quizzed and jotted as we went. My findings follow, arranged alphabetically as *aperçus* for the hard of reading, and amounting to an illustrated coffee-table book, or TV tie-out, shortly to subsume other English travel books by such as H. V. Morton, the little royal biographer.

Esher, May 1993

Abstractions: We English famously eschew abstractions. You'll find them on the Continent, of course. In France, they bandy abstractions *alfresco* in the afternoon. Abstractions and Merrie England are chalk and cheese, as Lady Finchley was the first to see. Confronted in Cabinet by an abstraction, she characteristically blew her top.

'Society?' she stormed. 'There's no such thing!'

I reminded young Partridge of this as we drove one day between Baldock and somewhere else on an English afternoon. The boy gave me an argument, of course.

'Your friend Enoch Powell might not agree,' he said. 'He deals frequently in abstractions – a particular favourite being the concept of the nation.'

'And what's wrong with that?' I said.

'It doesn't exist,' he said. 'Not in the Thatcherite sense, at least. You couldn't park it in your garage, nor, were national guilt the issue, could you put it in the dock. It's a logical construction and as such cannot be ostensively defined since predicates ascribed to it cannot be significantly ascribed to the entities from which it is constructed.' (*See* EDUCATION, THE USELESSNESS OF HIGHER.)

'Anything left of the pork pie, Mrs Root?' I said. I was playing for time, giving the boy enough rope to hang himself.

'The Japanese nation,' the boy said, 'is larger than the Swedish nation, but individual Japanese are smaller than individual Swedes. Equally, the cheery inhabitants of Merrie England, to whom you frequently refer, might have been apple-cheeked, but Merrie England itself couldn't sensibly be described as apple-cheeked.'

Here was a poser. If I had him correctly, the boy was alleging that Merrie England was a mere abstraction, that as such it didn't exist. If so, my people at Central Television had sprung a million in pursuit of a philosophical disaster. I puzzled it out, shortly confounded the boy by reference to Hasselblad and strobe.

'There is a difference,' I said, 'between such as the Hasselblad can catch and such as it can't. "Liberty" or "Patriotism" might defeat it, but I could pose a cheery blacksmith, the village idiot, a varlet and an apple-cheeked maiden round a maypole, later captioning the print as "Merrie England". As Dr Johnson had it: "Abstract liberty, like other mere abstractions, is not to be found." He made no reference, you'll note, to "Merrie England".'

'Berk,' I heard the boy say.

I clipped him round the ear.

'I was referring to Burke, the Tory thinker,' he said.

'I dare say you were,' I said. 'How about this, however, from Sir Gummer, the patriotic theologian? "I have every confidence that we English can protect ourselves against Continental ideas in general and abstract ideas in particular." And so we can. Did Henry V at Agincourt confront the haughty little Dauphin with abstractions? Not by a long chalk. It was two English fingers up and an arrow in the eye.'

'In fact,' said the boy, 'the archers at Agincourt were Welsh. I have that on the authority of Germaine Greer.'

'The big Australian? Went through the sixties without her underwear? I'd be inclined to take her views on archery with a pinch of salt. I'll have that pork pie now, Mrs Root.'

I find the appetite agreeably sharpened by the cut and thrust of abstract discourse.

Academics: In England, I'm glad to say, we take academics as we find them, referring to them as 'boffins' at best, at worst as arid intellectuals.

In France, needless to say, members of the so-called *Académie Française* take precedence – in placement at a *thé dansant*, say – over royalty, cardinals, diplomats and television personalities. Were Her Majesty to attend a *thé dansant* in Paris with a member of the *Académie*, she'd find herself below the salt. Further, members of the *Académie* have greater powers of entry than VAT inspectors in the UK, being entitled to run through your lounge-room at any time to correct your taste or syntax.

The only folk in England with greater powers than VAT inspectors are members of the hunt. Huntsmen, by medieval statute, are empowered to ride across your front garden at any time and demand, by the same medieval statute, a bucket of fox's offal with which to enrage their hounds and, for themselves, a yard of ale. (*See* HUNT, THE.)

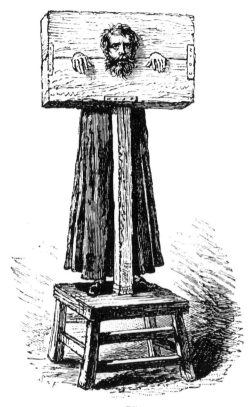

The Pillory.

Academics: A medieval Cambridge academic finds himself pilloried as a structuralist. So-called Terry Eagleton, the little Marxist and purveyor of 'isms' from abroad, can count himself lucky he was born too late for Merrie England.

We were driving to Grantchester along the leafy lanes, so I tagged the occasion with a felicitous line.

'"And is there honey still for tea . . . ?"' I cried. 'The dreaming spires. The Bridge of Sighs. The Backs, is it? We'll call on Archer, the little sprinter, visit "Dadie" Rylands in his rooms. The Fifth Man, was he?'

'I think we're in Oxford, Henry,' said Mrs Root.

'I dare say we are,' I said. 'And a good thing too. I never cared for Cambridge. Too flat, do you see? A cold wind from the Urals blowing abstract ideas clean down King's Parade. We won't stay long.'

'But we're not *in* Cambridge, Henry.'

'I'm delighted to hear it, Mrs Root. Pederasts and doctors for the most part. More recently cabaret comedians. Theorists. Structuralists. Isms and perversions. You'd not have found isms and perversions in Merrie England. Had you suggested in Merrie England that literature could as well be studied through the graffiti scrawled on a toilet wall as in the great works of our literary heritage (which is now being suggested in Cambridge, needless to say) you'd have found yourself arse up over a whipping block, I'll wager. You'll pardon my Merrie English, Mrs Root.

'Oxford, on the other hand, has always understood that the English academic is at his best in conversation over port or in the composition of the medium-length *éloge*. Sir Berlin, I gather, having dictated an *éloge*, then caught the train to London, where it was his agreeable custom to give his tutorials at the Ritz Hotel. What could be more English than that?'

'He isn't English,' said the boy Partridge.

'I'll be the judge of that,' I said. 'Either way, we'll visit him in his rooms. This won't take long.'

Nor did it, since he wasn't there. Most likely, he was taking his tea at the Ritz. At this point, and having done the Academy, I judged, I suggested that we take tea ourselves.

'Couldn't we see the House?' said Mrs Root.

'What house?' I said.

'Christ Church,' she said.

'Plenty of time for that,' I said. 'It'll not go away.'

Alas the woman had acquired a picture-book – *My Oxford* by Roger Scruton, the little Tory huntsman – of the sort which this volume will soon supplant. 'At least we could visit the Trout Inn by Godstow Bridge,' she said. 'It says here that "Generations have filled the place with laughter and talk, with exuberance and a youthful extravagance of mind, so that I do not know whether the old house or the people who run it are responsible for the impression that it is a quaint repository of much that is precious and lovable in the English character, among which I mention humour, tolerance and a casual acceptance of eccentricity." '

I was grateful for the warning. 'Thank you, Mrs Root,' I said. 'We'll give that one a miss. An English eccentric on an empty stomach is not my favourite prospect. Buttonholed by Rumpole of the Bailey in the Snug Bar? A blizzard of stuff by Wordsworth? I can do without that, thank you very much. Ah – this will do.'

We had entered a quaint, old-time tearoom, run by two mad biddies

on Parker's Nose, or possibly Parson's Piece; an establishment of the
sort which, if my friend Booker of the *Telegraph* is to be believed, is
under threat from Brussels. If so, a good thing too, since the service
offered by the biddies was deplorable and their home-made scones
compared unfavourably with Mr Kipling's individual Bakewell tarts.
(*See also* BIDDIES, MAD OLD.)

Action, World In: Trial by television. A fat man in gym-shoes
with hand-held camera inferring on air against defaulters, not least
the Old Bill.

We're on a slippery slope here, as that great, and essentially
English, jurist, Lord Denning, has constantly averred.

It's for the Old Bill to infer and an accredited judge or registrar
in chambers to send you up the Swannee.

We can be grateful at least to my friend Marcus Plantin – the new
ITV scheduling supremo – who has recently announced his intention
to axe such as *World In Action*.

'It is not the job of television,' he said, 'to get innocent men
out of prison.'

Hear hear to that, I say. It is, however, the Old Bill's to put
them in there. (*See also* DENNING, LORD; JUSTICE, BRITISH; *and*
SLOPES, SLIPPERY.)

Advisers, Financial: Until recently, a financial adviser worked
in the City and took an overview of your portfolio. Nowadays,
he's a bald American, as often as not, who spends his after hours
cuckolding the House of Windsor, not least the Duke of York.

You'd not find the manager of my own portfolio, Sir Hambro,
of Hambros, doing that. You'd not drop in on Hambros, doff the
bowler, shoot the cuff, inform the lass in the vestibule that you
wanted Sir Hambro to spring a wedge from the Scottish Widows,
only to be told that he was out at the moment, cuckolding the House
of Windsor.

Time was when a monarch's son wouldn't have been cuckolded
by a bald American. Had you cuckolded a monarch's son in Merrie
England, you'd have been turned on a spit at best, at worst been sat
on a spike in public. But the bald American who cuckolded York
seems to have fallen on his feet and may, indeed, participate in the
Ferguson woman's pay-off. (*See also* PRINCE ANDREW.)

Financial Advisers: Times change. Until quite recently, the chap in charge of your portfolio wore a pinstripe suit and bowler hat, as per young Sir Hambro (*left*). His probity was as starched as his laundered shirt. Now, like John Bryan, the little Texan (*right*), he'll appear in public in his vest and, in his leisure hours, he'll destabilise the House of Windsor.

Agincourt: *See* ABSTRACTIONS; *and* FALSTAFF, JACK.

Aldermen: You'll not have read *An English Journey* by my friend 'Dick' West. It'll be out of print, I take it. You've not missed much. That said, he does provide therein a list of the worst innovations of the last twenty-five years – among them, the Arts Council; commercial TV and radio; one-day cricket; abortion on demand; the EEC; the Race Relations Act; and the abolition of aldermen.

I'd not go along with him on the demise of aldermen. An alderman is a jack-in-office locally, and it is my misfortune to have an ex-alderman as my next-door neighbour here in Esher – Major Entwistle (rtd) to be precise. Reluctant as I am to intrude myself into a rigorously objective account of Merrie England, I feel I must.

The fact is I have a running *contretemps* on my hands. Like many semi-retired men in Esher, I plan to add an extension to my house – to be precise, a games room with bar and snooker accoutrements for when the boys come round – but find myself constantly baulked by Entwistle when seeking the appropriate permissions.

Mention of Entwistle will inevitably occur from time to time, though I'll not take advantage of my platform here to call the man a horse. That's not my way. (*See also* ENTWISTLE, ALDERMAN.)

Allegations: Always 'unsubstantiated', not least when levelled against the Old Bill. Thus, two black teenagers – subsequently known as the Highbury Two – who had dragged nine of our community police out of a transit van and given them a kicking, later made the 'unsubstantiated' allegation that the assault had in fact been vice versa.

Allegations: A very English scene. A community bobby on the beat questions a member of the public in order to eliminate him from his enquiries.

No true Englishman would issue an unsubstantiated allegation, though a self-pitying Scot or neurotic Welshman might. (*See* SCRUM, COLLAPSING THE.) Provided he has funds at his disposal, the Englishman, since Magna Carta, has always had access to the British legal system, can instruct a barrister in chambers. Without funds, an Englishman's recourse is to lead with the knuckle and stand up close, to breathe down his opponent's neck. They don't like you breathing down their necks – least of all jacks-in-office such as aldermen.

Allen, Dave: *See* ICONOCLASM, ACCEPTABLE.

Amateur, The Gifted: Time was when every cricketing county was captained by a Gifted Amateur, recently one of 'The Few' in World War Two and distinguishable from the mere 'professionals' under his command by dint of his haughty mien and the fact that he couldn't play for toffee. Lord Hawke, was it? 'Plum' Warner? He was one. B. R. 'Bunny' Valentine of Kent another.

The Gifted Amateur: 'How's that?!?' Time was when an English test team never forgot that cricket was a game to be enjoyed. Here, that true Corinthian, Denis Compton (c. Evans, b. Trueman, 4!) has a practice net before facing Lindwall and Miller at Lords in '48.

By contrast, some 'professionals', though they parted their hair in the middle and wore an excess of Brylcreem at the wicket, were 'gifted amateurs' – definable as such, and in spite of being on a modest weekly wage, by their nonchalant attitude at the popping crease.

It would do the boy no harm, I thought, to learn about the Gifted Amateur, so driving to Dover one day to check our frontiers against the influx of abstract ideas and trans-Continental drug-fiends (with a woman in charge at VAT and Excise it behoves us all to be alert), I expatiated on the subject.

'The concept,' I said, 'originates in cricket before the war – the gentleman as against the player – but soon had wider application. In films of the time, such as Sir Leslie Howard and David Niven – confounding foreigners with insouciance and *badinage* – displayed the unhurried characteristics of the Gifted Amateur. Modesty. Aplomb. A suggestion of rhythm in the waltz. A feeling that they could see off Johnnie Frenchman with both hands tied behind their backs.

'Sir Donat, he was another. Up to his eyes in wet bracken and padlocked to a foreign actress, but retaining his *sang-froid* none the less. *The Thirty-Nine Steps*, was it? They don't make films like that any more. Now it's gratuitous sex scenes, all too often featuring the one built like a billiard ball. Bob Hoskins at a guess. Where was I?'

'Cricket, Mr Root,' said the boy.

'Well done. Time was when the Gifted Amateur prevailed. C. B. Fry jumped for England on the morning of his Oxford finals; took a first; then scored a double century between tea at the Ritz and cocktails at the Café Royal. After the war, the amateurs toiled their way to 3 not out in an afternoon, leaving it to the "professionals" at the other end to flash their bats.

'Denis Compton. He was one. Against Australia in '48, Compton came to the wicket in black tie and dancing pumps, and carrying a bat he'd borrowed from a schoolboy. England were 109 for 5 and Miller and Lindwall had their tails up. No one gave England a chance. A *professional* professional might have let the pressure get to him, but Compton displayed the true spirit of the Gifted Amateur. He was bowled first ball.'

'Sir Garfield Sobers?' said the boy. 'Was he a Gifted Amateur?'

'Certainly not,' I said. 'He was a Calypso Cavalier and as such couldn't, either by definition or pigmentation, have been a Gifted Amateur. Sir Donat in black face, padlocked to a foreign actress and up to his eyes in wet bracken, would have created quite the wrong impression.

'A Calypso Cavalier can display Natural Talent, but that's an entirely different matter. We English frown on Natural Talent, preferring press-ups and bed in a dormitory by 10 p.m. Hence the debate as to the respective merits of the lad Gower and the portly soprano, Gooch. The lad Gower has Natural Talent, displaying nonchalance outside the off-stump and discussing last night's wine list in the slips. We'll not want that at the Mecca of cricket. We'll not want a discussion of last night's wine list in the slips.'

As luck would have it, I spotted a poster as we drove through Canterbury advertising the fact that the men of Kent were currently at home to Hampshire.

'We'll drop in and see the lad Gower,' I said.

Alas, he was out for nought before we got there.

'Oh good,' said Mrs Root. 'We can visit the cathedral.'

'Speak for yourself, Mrs Root,' I said.

Plenty of time for that after we'd checked on the little woman in charge at VAT and Excise. It'd not go away. (*See also* CATHEDRAL, CANTERBURY; *and* COACHING.)

Amsterdam, The Latest Evidence from: The true Englishman ignores the latest evidence from Amsterdam. (*See also* DRUNK, THE ENGLISH.)

Anglais, Le Vice: See BASQUES.

Areas, No-Go: Passing through the City one day, on the way to the East End, young Partridge and I had a most fruitful discussion in the matter of that most un-English of new phenomena, no-go areas. Time was, I said, when you could go anywhere in London. Not any more. In Stoke Newington and parts of Brixton, twelve-year-olds carry pump-action shotguns and stick each other up for a packet of Smarties.

'Inner city deprivation,' Partridge said.

I was ready for this, of course. 'Don't give me inner-city deprivation,' I said. 'In my neck of the woods – the East End of London – it was three to the shirt and the outside bucket, but had a toff come down that way we'd not have had his wallet. We'd have had his hub-caps, and serve him right. Poor but respectable, that was us. Able to distinguish between right and wrong. Never mind social conditions, young Partridge; it's straightforward wickedness we're up against; that most unfashionable notion, original sin.'

The boy hadn't had enough. 'I suppose you're right,' he said. 'Only an irredeemable logic-chopper would find it problematic that original sin is distributed so much more widely in Stoke Newington and Brixton than in Belgrave Square and Esher.'

Irony, was it? I'd not have that. I'd not have irony on page 21 of a travel book, and I clipped him round the ear.

'If you go on clipping him round the ear,' said Mrs Root, 'you'll find yourself on the wrong end of a caring hot-line.'

She was right about that and no mistake, so I resorted to theology.

'God moves in a mysterious way,' I said.

'Oh look,' said Mrs Root. 'St Paul's Cathedral. Can we drop in?'

'Plenty of time for that later,' I said. 'It'll not go away.'

Art, Subsidised: Strolling through the once agreeable market town of Norwich on an English summer afternoon, we were confronted suddenly by two chalk-faced art students covered in beads and holding poles.

'What's this, Rodney?' I said to one of the chalk-faced mimes.

'Community art,' he said.

I gave him community art. I seized his pole and jousted him arse over beads into the river.

Later, over a Big 'Un in McDonalds, I expatiated for the sake of Mrs Root.

'Community art indeed!' I said. 'Obscenity on the rates, as often as not – or it would be, were the rates still appertaining. Verses that don't rhyme. Six skinny women in a garage offering Sapphic exchanges as lunchtime theatre. Small wonder that when my friend Sir Isaacs, the little opera buff and general arts aficionado, visited the Tate the other day he hung his hat on one of the exhibits. Sir Isaacs is more *au fait* than some, so where might others hang their hats?

'And I'll tell you something further, Mrs Root. Bill Shakespeare didn't need a grant. He was a popular playwright in the best sense of the word, needing neither crib nor hand-out. The rude groundlings took his drift. "To be, or not to be . . ." They led the laughter.'

'I see the local theatre is showing *Carousel*,' said Mrs Root.

' "You'll Never Walk Alone"?' I said. ' "This Was A Real Nice Clambake"? "When I Marry Mr Snow"? I'd rather see the six skinny

Sapphists in a garage, thank you very much.'

Mrs Root was not confounded. 'But you like a musical, Henry,' she said.

'Only those by my friend Sir Webber, the balloon-faced cellist,' I said. 'The large ballads with a patriotic underthump and an indigenous theme.'

'I see,' said Mrs Root. 'Like "Don't Cry For Me, Argentina"?'

'Have another Big 'Un, Mrs Root,' I said.

Background: Here's a conundrum: why can some become English while others can't? Moira Shearer, the little newscaster, seems to have settled in, whereas Lord Palumbo, once of the Arts Council and Centre Point, still smacks to me of the pampas, hacienda and scarlet cummerbund. One could envisage him doing the tango at a tea dance.

That said, where better to puzzle the matter out than the Snug Bar of the Admiral Nelson, Chingford, whither I'd come on a summer afternoon with the boy Partridge and Mrs Root – our assignment being to research the lower middle classes.

The backbone of England, Mrs Root, I'd said. Lady Finchley's people. Delayed gratification. One's ambitions achieved once one's six feet under. Access paid, the mortgage likewise. We'd not stay long, I'd said. At which point, who should I spot yarning informally with mine host but Lord Tebbit of Chingford himself.

'Argue me this, Chingford,' I said. 'Why can some become English while others can't? Sir Worsthorne, the little Dutchman, has made the switch – has acquired an acceptably beefy prose style, some would say – whereas Imran Kahn, the proud little Pakistani cricketer, is still to be seen in discos such as Tramp wearing an ethnic skirt. You'd not see Sir Worsthorne down Tramp wearing an ethnic skirt.'

'We're off the record?' Chingford said.

'Of course,' I said, instructing the boy *sotto voce* to turn the sound up on his portable recorder. We in the field of docudrama never go off the record. *Caveat respondee*, as the Latins had it. My obligations were entirely to the fat man in Birmingham with the cheque book. If Chingford made a prime-time monkey of himself, *tant pis*.

Chingford scratched his nose and pondered for a while, shortly pronouncing that it had to do with background.

'You can't put old wine into old bottles,' he said. 'Your Asian, like your Gaul or Latin, has too much background. On the other . . .'

I held a hand up. Once on their hind legs, these politicos will ramble on unless you stop them.

'Hold hard,' I said. 'You're suggesting that the Dutch have a certain amount of background – albeit as art forgers for the most part – but on moving here are happy to eschew it? Hence Sir Worsthorne? Is that your drift?'

'I'm saying that . . .'

'Whereas your little Asian, Gaul or Latin carries an excess of cultural baggage and cannot – even after living here for many years – respond in his water as an Englishman? The large ballooning ballad by Sir Lloyd Webber, the little cellist, leaves him cold? Asians, Gauls and Latins fail to respond correctly to *Pomp And Circumstance* by that most convivial of English composers, Sir Edward Elgar? Is that what you're saying? The floor is yours.'

'I'm saying that they won't . . .'

'. . . assimilate. Is that it? You're inferring that your Pakistani invades the pitch and jostles Dickie Bird. I'm with you here. No true Englishman would jostle Dickie Bird. Nor, I may say, would an Australian. Your Australian, having no background of his own, soon picks up our ways and settles in, once he has removed the chip from his shoulder *in re* his own cultural shortcomings.'

'That's right,' said Chingford. 'Your Australian will stand on his own two feet and, rather than be a drain on our hard-pressed social services, will help himself.'

'You're telling me,' I said. 'The newly arrived Australian characteristically disguises himself as an enormous poacher's pocket and runs in and out of stores in Oxford Street. Better, I suppose, than relying on hand-outs from the nanny state.'

Chingford chuckled briefly, like an ancient gate wheezing on its hinge.

'A good example of the Enterprise Culture in operation,' he said.

That settled, Chingford and I shared a ploughman's lunch, reflected that there was little wrong with England while scenes like this survived. Men in weekend jumpers from Marks & Spencers standing in thin sunshine, holding tall lagers and discussing cars. Their failed wives quacking about underfelt in little groups. Fat five-year-olds clutching fizzy drinks. Easy-on-the-ear selections piped from a karaoke. There was no one here who'd wear an ethnic skirt in Tramp, invade the pitch at Lord's or jostle Dickie Bird.

Shortly thereafter, Chingford excused himself and made for his

Fiesta family hatchback, only to discover that one of the tyres was flat. While changing it, he looked up to discover that a man in a weekend jumper was head-down under the bonnet.

'Here!' cried Chingford. 'What's your game?'

'If you're having the wheels, I'm having the battery,' the fellow said.

I had to laugh. 'The Enterprise Culture in operation!' I said. 'You'd better get on your bike!'

Chingford was unamused. I don't know why. (*See also* ELGAR, SIR EDWARD; *and* HERITAGE, ENGLISH.

Barbecues: Green-belt Englishmen such as myself have taken to the barbecue party as ducks to water. That's why I'd hitherto believed that this mode of entertaining originated not in Australia, as some suppose, but in medieval England, where those of yeoman stock roasted a pig alfresco on a spit, thereafter holding a wassail through the night.

Such was my thinking. Imagine my surprise, therefore, when on returning to Esher after an investigative sortie to the Mendips (we'd not stayed long), I said that we'd celebrate the success of our research to date with a barbecue party on the lawn – only to be greeted by a brief dismissive snigger from the boy Partridge and the assertion that barbecue parties are for suburban types who read the *Mail On Sunday*.

'I'm surprised at you, Mr Root,' he said. 'A group of men, who haven't been inside a kitchen for twenty years, wearing facetious aprons and arguing over the merits of competing firelighters! It will be a wok from Peter Jones next and cheese fondues on the terrace.'

You could have knocked me down with a feather, frankly – not least because a wok from Peter Jones was currently on order. I was lost for words, only recovered my wits when Alderman Entwistle (rtd) popped his head above the adjoining privet hedge and asked me to keep the noise down on Saturday night since he'd invited Esher's social 'A' list – Michael Aspel, Sir Robert and Lady Mark and so forth – to a barbecue party on his lawn.

I kept my head. 'Up yours, Entwistle,' I said. 'Barbecues are for suburban types who read the *Mail On Sunday*. It will be a wok from Peter Jones next and fondues on the terrace! I'm grateful for the warning, but will not be at home that night. I'll be at Blenheim, as it happens, calling on my friend Lord Bath . . .'

At this point, I was interrupted by the boy. 'Marlborough, Mr Root,' he said.

'Thank you, Partridge. I'll be in Bath, calling on my friend, Lord Marlborough. Either way, I'd be surprised to find his Lordship holding a barbecue on his lawn – still more so to discover that Sir Mark and his lady were fellow guests. The last time Lady Mark visited a stately home, she was mistaken for Thora Hird and redirected to the *artistes'* entrance. Have a pleasant evening.'

As I've said before, I'll not take advantage of my platform here to infer against Alderman Entwistle (rtd) as was; suffice it to say that he's always struck me as the sort of man who'd don a facetious apron and hold a barbecue on his lawn for others of his suburban ilk. (*See also* ENTWISTLE, ALDERMAN; *and* HOMES, STATELY.)

Basques: No respectable English woman – least of all a Tory MP's wife – would have any business with a *basque* (I refer here to the Continental undergarment, not to the little north Spanish revolutionaries.) A Tory wife, however, customarily stands by her husband after he's been entrapped in a West Kensington apartment by a foreign 'actress' wearing one; and will thereafter appear in the tabloids at his side in Wellington boots and smiling bravely.

David Mellor, was it? The little ex-Minister for English Heritage and so forth? You can't blame the man. Nothing in our culture had prepared him for the sight of a foreign 'actress' in a *basque*. An Englishman, unaccustomed to seeing a woman in a *basque*, is immediately undone. His breathing becomes heavy. He deliquesces. He forgets his responsibilities in Cabinet and poses arse up over the foreign lady's knee. Nothing wrong with that. Naval tradition, nothing more.

I wonder, however, whether the time has come to weaken our hitherto adamantine attitude to *basques*. With our frontiers coming down (in spite of the new woman at VAT and Excise's assurances that under her a constant SAS presence will remain on the *qui vive* against rabies, abstract ideas and trans-Continental drug fiends), I can't help feeling that there will be an influx of foreign 'actresses' in *basques* – with, as a consequence, an upsurge in the number of Englishmen entrapped in West Kensington and elsewhere.

In the circumstances, might it not be the lesser evil if Lord Rees-Mogg, who is in charge of morals *in re* television, were to allow a certain amount of foreign erotica – women in *basques* and so forth – to be beamed to us in our English lounge-rooms? Thus, we would become accustomed to seeing our women and servants so attired – the upshot being a diminution in Tory Party scandals.

Travelling through Somerset one day – in search of blacksmiths, Anglo-Catholics, village idiots etc – I dropped in on Rees-Mogg, meaning to discuss the matter on the spot. Alas, he wasn't there. (*See also* DE SANCHA, ANTONIA; KEELER, CHRISTINE; *and* LAMBTON, LORD.)

Bath: On our journey through Somerset, in search of village idiots and so forth, Mrs Root said, quite clearly:

'Bath is the dear old lady of Somerset: grey-haired, mittened, smelling faintly of lavender; one of those old ladies who have lived a much-discussed past, and are as obviously respectable as only old ladies with crowded pasts can be.'

Bath: The famous city of Bath, celebrated for its crescents and so forth since the days when 'Beau' Nash, the little dandy, came here for a medicinal tubbing in 1706 and put it on the tourist map. Owing to a legislative anomaly, it is a statutory offence to walk a dog across the Royal Crescent on the last Tuesday of every month.

'Do what, Mrs Root?' I said.

'I'm quoting from *England Anthologised*,' she said, 'by Sir Kenneth Baker.'

'The little Tory versifier?' I said. 'Well I'd thank you not to. Not on an empty stomach' – but I couldn't stem the woman's flow.

' "She nurses you," ' she said, ' "with a shrewd twinkle in which you detect experience mellowed by age. You look at her lovingly, wondering how she could ever have been so wicked; wishing that she could be young again for one wild evening! Oh gracious old lady of Somerset, how I love to be nursed at your once haughty knee!" '

'Thank you, Mrs Root,' I said. 'We'll give Bath a miss, I think.' And so we did.

Battle Abbey: It might seem baffling to a foreigner that the place where our national destiny was sealed should be devoted to the education of – of all things! – women.

For here, if anywhere, is a sacred national shrine, yet when you approach the gateway to Battle Abbey – as I, Mrs Root and the boy Partridge did on an English summer afternoon – it is soon made clear to you that Battle Abbey is a girls' school first and a national shrine a long way after.

Battle Abbey: On the site where Harold got it in the eye, a girls' school stands — albeit one lacking in amenities. So far, the Roof Restoration Fund, launched by the Board of Governors and a consortium of *alumni* and parents, seems not to have been very well supported.

As every schoolboy knows (*see* EDUCATION, THE USELESSNESS OF HIGHER), Battle Abbey was built by William the Conqueror and was later pulled down by order of Henry VIII. A boring old gatekeeper, however, will show you an illuminated parchment, which contains the names of those who came over with the Conqueror.

'You'll not be on it, Partridge,' I said. 'You smack of *arrivisme* if anyone did.'

Nor was he, but glancing down the scroll I saw my own name sure enough – *Baron Henri de la Rue of Harfleur.*

'Oh dear, *Monsieur de la Rue,*' said the boy. 'That means I'm more English than you are. No wonder you don't fit in in Esher. Too much background.' (*See also* BACKGROUND.)

I wasn't lost for a riposte. I clipped him round the ear.

Beaumont, Billy: *See* GIANTS, GENTLE.

Bicycle, The Humble: The humble bicycle has a role to play in two current and appertaining issues. Thanks to my friend Lord Chingford's celebrated injunction to the unemployable, it has received illustrative mention in monetarist debates. Plus, and more importantly, it signifies the difference between the English conception of the Monarchy and that obtaining on the Continent.

We'll not want our Monarch trooping the colour on a bicycle, as per lesser monarchs in other parts. The bicycle suits the Dutch monarch, not the English. It's a question of mystique, as has been observed by such as Lord St John of Fawsley, the little constitutionalist. The Dutch monarch lacks mystique; is customarily to be seen pedalling through a shopping mall in jeans. We'll not want that here. We'll not want our Monarch pedalling through a shopping mall with groceries fore and aft.

To illustrate my point, I arranged for Mrs Root, the boy and myself to see the colour trooped on an English summer afternoon. I tapped a tourist on the shoulder.

'As you can see,' I said, 'the English Monarch is most appropriately conveyed by horse. If you placed the Dutch monarch side-saddle on a horse, she'd swing through one hundred and eighty degrees and hit the deck on the other side, that's my guess. Where do you come from, by the way?'

'Amsterdam,' he said.

'In that case,' I said, 'you'll know what I mean.'

The Humble Bicycle (1):
When Lord Hailsham, a
true Englishman, was re-
placed on the Woolsack
by, of all things, a Scot —
one Lord Mackay, of that
ilk — did he moan and
whimper and talk of social
deprivation? No, he got on
his bike and went in search
of alternative employment.

The Humble Bicycle (2):
Trooping the Colour
annually provides Her
Majesty the Queen with an
opportunity to display a
very English skill: a proper
carriage on a horse. In fact,
Her Majesty is nailed by
the buttocks to a surgical
saddle attached to the
horse's rump. A similar
device, incidentally, pre-
vents her dropping off
during my friend Lord
Delfont's annual Royal
Variety Show.

Biddies, Mad Old: Time was when every English village had two mad old biddies – often sisters, one with a wart – who ran a tearoom and, in their after hours, cured adder's bite and giddiness in cattle.

Such establishments are, as previously mentioned, under threat from faceless bureaucrats in Brussels, the latter having ruled not only against the biddies' cure for adder's bite but also against their damson jam and scones.

'And a good thing too,' I said one day, as we returned from our research *in re* the academy. (See ACADEMICS.) 'And I know what I'm talking about, believe me. My own mother was a biddy, no doubt still is.'

Mrs Root seemed startled by the info. 'I didn't know your mother was still alive, Henry,' she said. 'Where is the dear old lady?'

'In a home,' I said. 'Popped her in there twenty years ago – haven't seen her since. We'll visit her. Tell her that she came over with the Conqueror. She'll be grateful for the news.'

And so she was, no doubt – once it had been conveyed to her. We pitched up at the home, entered a ward, approached a sleeping biddy in a bed.

I shook her awake, gave her my card. 'Henry Root, Wet Fish,' I said. 'I'm your son. Treating you well, are they? Here's the good news: it transpires we came over with the Conqueror. *Henri de la Rue of Harfleur.* In the circumstances, I'd pitch for a better bed, if I were you. This is the wife. Don't laugh.'

At this point, Matron told me that I was addressing myself to the wrong old biddy. Mine was two beds down, it seemed.

'I can't go through all that stuff again,' I said. 'I'm a busy man. In the next three weeks I've the whole of England to research for Central Television. I'd be obliged if you'd pass the info on.'

Then I left, as relieved as you'd have been to discover that your mad old mother was still extant. (*See also* BATTLE ABBEY.)

Blacksmith: As we drove through Wiltshire on the way to Salisbury, Mrs Root started to read from a travel book of the sort which this one will shortly incommode – *My Wiltshire*, by Sir Edward Heath, to be precise.

' "The blacksmith's forge is still alive in Pewsey," ' she said.

'Thank you for the info, Mrs Root,' I said. 'We'll give that a miss.'

Blacksmith: In the remote Mendips, an honest English blacksmith practises his dying craft. Once he doubled as village idiot and pharmacist. Alas, no longer. Now Boots the Chemist has a branch on every corner, while, at local fêtes, the role of village idiot is taken by a weekend visitor from London − as often as not by Lord Rees-Mogg.

Blandford, The Marquess of: As we drove to Blenheim one afternoon to call on my friend Lord Bath, the boy Partridge suddenly said:

'When we come to do the TV programme, Mr Root, I hope you won't mention the Marquess of Blandford. To do so would only add to the family's grief.'

A pleasure boat sunk in the Thames, was it? Turned turtle with all hands and sixty debutantes on board? Why would I mention that? It had nothing to do with my main theme − 'Merrie England − Whither?' − and I said as much to the boy.

'I'm not insensitive,' I said. 'I'd not make gratuitous reference in a prime-time slot to the participants in a human tragedy – least of all those who woke up in hospital to find Gloria Hunniford at their bedside quizzing them with hand-held mike. I'll tell you this, however. If I'd survived a ducking in the Thames, I'd be well pleased to find Gloria Hunniford at my bedside. I'd be relieved it wasn't Esther Rantzen.' (*See also* RANTZEN, ESTHER.)

'We're at cross purposes, Mr Root,' said Partridge. 'It was the *Marchioness* which sank in the Thames. I'm referring to the Marquess of Blandford, the Duke of Marlborough's troubled heir.'

That rang a bell. The victor at Quebec, unless I was much mistaken, and as mad as a March hare. Not that the tag bothered good Queen Anne. 'Would that he'd bite my other generals,' was her reaction.

'Small wonder the boy's in trouble,' I said. 'His ancestor, the victor at Quebec, was as mad as a hatter from all accounts.'

'That wasn't Marlborough,' said the boy. 'General Wolfe was the victor at Quebec.'

'I dare say he was,' I said, 'and all the more reason not to mention his boy to Marlborough.'

I'd not be the one to remind others yet again that young Blandford is a convicted dope fiend, that he once burgled his sister's handbag for pawnable trinkets with which to fund his habit, that on a later occasion he burst out of Boots in the middle of the night with a trolleyful of syringes, suppositories and worse. I'd not do that. (*See also* HOMES, STATELY.)

Boat Race, The: An essentially English institution. Where else in the world could such an apparently élitist annual confrontation arouse the passions of high and low, black and white?

Once a year, humble Indian shopkeepers don a rosette of appropriate hue and mingle with their betters on the towpath. Ancient wet bobs in prep-school caps, their heads no bigger than a grapefruit, follow the race on bicycles, while still grander ex-participants – old blues and so forth – keep their distance in a convoy of launches and throw lobster carcasses at humble supporters on the bank. A very English scene.

I hired a launch myself this year, took the boy along, marked his card *in re* the likely outcome.

'This year,' I said, 'Cambridge are in with a real chance. The pressure's all on Oxford.'

The Boat Race: The chickens come home to roost. The Cambridge eight sinks under a weight of barren 'isms' from abroad; a semiologist at stroke cracks heads with a deconstructionalist at two; arguments break out as to the merits of Barthes and Derrida. Meanwhile, the urbane, metropolitan Oxford eight opens the picnic hamper and coasts to another easy victory.

At the first bend, Cambridge were three lengths down. Oxford took their water. I was unconcerned. I can read a race. 'Cambridge are pacing themselves,' I told the boy. Shortly thereafter, the Oxford stroke lit his first cigarette of the race, the crew began to point out historical landmarks to one another. Morale collapsed in the Cambridge boat. They were twelve lengths down, quarrels broke out, heads cracked together as rhythm went. Bow caught a crab. Cambridge sank.

I can take a joke against myself. I hit the boy. (*See also* CHEATING.)

Boffins: The French have thinkers, we have boffins – sometimes eggheads – either term conjuring up an agreeably comic image of a mad character without socks and with a panto hairstyle.

Expatiating on boffins one day for the benefit of the boy, I observed that Malcolm Muggeridge got it right for once when he incomparably observed that 'it wasn't Hitler or Stalin or John Foster Dulles who invented the atomic bomb, but a rum-looking boffin – one Albert Einstein – scribbling on a bit of paper.'

'Muggeridge is dead,' said the boy, though what that had to do with it I can't imagine.

'And about time too,' I said. 'I never cared for him. He was an iconoclast, do you see? We English frown on iconoclasts, though we do have them, of course. Dawn and Saunders, is it? The *Daily Telegraph* speaks for England, not Dawn and Saunders. Where was I?'

'Boffins, Mr Root.'

Boffins: To confuse her lover, Dame Redgrave – appearing here as Isadora Duncan – dances in the Greek mode, and in a nightdress fashioned out of tea towels. Duncan died tragically in an automobile accident – like so many foreign intellectuals.

'Well done. In films dealing with World War Two, boffins were customarily enacted by Sir Michael Redgrave as mad old parties who used their brains in the interests of a practical outcome – such as designing a bouncing bomb to drop on Germany.'

How ironic, incidentally, that Sir Redgrave's offspring went the other way. Corin a Marxist, Vanessa dancing in a tea towel on a lawn as Isadora Duncan. We can be grateful that Sir Redgrave didn't live to see it. (*See also* ICONOCLASM, ACCEPTABLE; MOORE, PATRICK; *and* SCIENTISTS.)

Broadstairs: *See* HOLIDAY, THE ENGLISH SUMMER.

Buffs: An Englishman can, without giving offence, be a buff – never a *cinéphile*. My friend, Michael Parkinson, for instance, is a buff. If you visit his delightful house in Maidenhead, you'll spot memorabilia there *in re* his days as a buff – enlarged likenesses of such as Humphrey Bogart, Cyd Charisse and Virginia Mayo. Further, he and his wife, Mary, sometimes on a Friday night, roll back the carpet and enact routines from *Singing In The Rain* or, if you're out of luck, the final scene from *Casablanca*. (*See also* NORMAN, BARRY.)

Bullying: During a lull in our research, I expatiated one day – for the benefit of the boy and Mrs Root – on the subject of public schools.

'Bump suppers, Mrs Root,' I said. 'Boys in boaters. Perverts in charge. At Winchester, I'm told, the boys bathe in the buff in Gunners Hole – a patch of river cordoned off. Too late, young Partridge, they closed last week.'

We'd visit the place in Cloister Time, I said, check on whether the fine old tradition of bullying still prevailed. On their first day, new boys, I'm told, are parcelled up in laundry skips and tobogganed down a stairwell. Later, in the library, prefects suspend them on toasting forks and kebab their backsides.

'It all sounds very brutal,' said Mrs Root.

'Nonsense,' I said. 'How else is a boy to acquire *sang-froid* and a sense of humour or, as a defence, build up the lonely, introspective habits of a playwright? Nine out of ten of our leading playwrights were bullied at public school, I'm told. Rumpole of the Bailey became a playwright after his toy panda was ceremonially decapitated at Winchester by some celebrating rugger buggers.'

'As it happens, they don't play rugger at Winchester,' said the boy, 'and Rumpole of the Bailey, as you call him, went to Harrow.'

'I dare say he did,' I said. 'We'll visit Winchester none the less.'

'Oh good,' said Mrs Root. 'We can see the Cathedral.'

'On second thoughts,' I said. 'We'll go to Eton.'

'Oh good,' said Mrs Root. 'We can visit Windsor Castle. It's a depository of our history, from all I've heard.'

'We'll go to Harrow after all,' I said. (*See also* ETON; *and* FEAST, AGAR'S.)

Carnival, The Notting Hill: An offence to all true Englishmen. I'll be a Dutchman if it wasn't Alexander Chancellor, the *Spectator*'s relaxed ex-Editor, who wrote:

'The ghastly Notting Hill Carnival, the annual festival of London's West Indians, took place last weekend. Respectable householders in the neighbourhood stayed at home to protect their property, with the disagreeable consequence that they missed their country house weekends.'

That says it all. For safety's sake, shopkeepers black up in woolly wigs. In a shameful attempt to integrate, heavy-footed policemen hand-jive with drug-crazed street thieves, smoke ganja in Rastafarian churches. Roy Hattersley limbo dances competitively with the Bottomley woman. The Prince of Wales, concerned that he may one day be hung by the heels from a lamppost and spat at by disaffected subjects, attends in a Hawaiian shirt and open-toed sandals.

Of a mind to don body armour and, for research purposes, to attend the thing, I exposited for the boy.

'A deplorable event,' I said. 'Imagine the outcry from the natives were a party of relocated Englishmen to erect a maypole in the jungle, thereafter dancing round it and singing patriotic songs. They'd be head first into the cooking pot, I tell you. When in Rome and so forth.'

I got an argument from the boy, of course. 'You are guilty of the relativist fallacy, Mr Root,' he said. ' "When in Rome . . ." is at best a piece of advice in the field of social etiquette. In philosophy it is the logically disastrous attachment of a non-relative morality of tolerance ("do as others do") to a view of morality as relative. As Bernard Williams had it: "It cannot be a consequence of morality that a society, confronted with the practice of another, ought, if rational, to react with acceptance. To draw these consequences is the characteristic, and inconsistent, step of vulgar relativism." ' (*See also* EDUCATION, THE USELESSNESS OF HIGHER.)

I was too quick for the lad. 'Precisely,' I said. 'Which is why I'll not countenance Caribbean practices on an English green. I suggest that your friend Sir Williams puts that where the monkey put its nuts. You'll pardon the philosophical vernacular, Mrs Root.'

Cat Burglar, The Cheery English: It is a sign of our national decline, surely, that cat burgling, as a profession, is dying out. The cheery English cat burglar knew his place – which, often as not, was up a chimney. Every street had a cat burglar. We had one. He never used the front door. It was a matter of professional pride. Ask him to tea, and he'd gain entry down the chimney.

On top of which, he respected his betters. On being fitted up by the Old Bill, he didn't shout the odds or make the usual allegations. 'It's a fair cop, guv,' he said.

Of a mind one day to research the disappearing English cat burglar, I dropped in on my neighbour, Sir Robert Mark, as was.

'Argue me this, Sir Mark,' I said. 'Weren't things better when the cheery cat burglar knew his place?'

'Root,' he said, 'you've hit the nail on the head. Today, it's ethnic crime wherever you look. Tongs and Triads coming through the privet hedge and pushing rice pudding through the letter-box. When I was a young copper on the beat there was mutual respect between the cat burglar and ourselves. On being questioned round the groin and kidneys, he didn't make the usual allegations. He did his porridge. What's that noise?'

While we'd been yarning downstairs, a cat burglar had gained entry down the chimney, thereafter having it away with Sir Mark's medals and spare TV. I had to laugh, but Sir Mark was far from pleased.

Castle: Since Magna Carta, an Englishman's home has, Lord Denning concurring, been his castle – as my next-door neighbour, ex-Alderman Entwistle, will shortly discover to his cost.

As I may have mentioned hitherto, I think, I have been of a mind of late to erect an extension to my house – more precisely, a games room for when the boys come round. A man and his pals don't want to be disturbed when yarning, by the sound of women quacking in the kitchen. Further, I may have mentioned that I've been constantly thwarted in this endeavour by Alderman Entwistle who, in his officious way, has sought to discover whether I have the relevant permissions.

Today he went too far. I came home from researching the Mendips (they'd not gone away) to discover that this little Hitler had called the District Surveyor in; worse, that the latter functionary had ruled that my games room must be dismantled.

I'll not have that. I'll not accept the dictates of a faceless local bureaucrat. I'm not a vindictive man, but I intend to initiate a campaign of vilification against the said Entwistle and his jack-in-office, the District Surveyor.

Swift, was it, the little polemicist? The *Dunciad* and the other one? 'Who breaks a butterfly upon a wheel'? I'll take a leaf from the little polemicist's book, issue lampoons against Entwistle, my tormentor. The pen is mightier than the sword. The Englishman will not be gagged. (*See also* ENTWISTLE, ALDERMAN.)

Cathedral, Canterbury: It's still there, I'm glad to say.

Chatterley, The Trial of Lady: As Lady Finchley constantly averred before her sad betrayal, we're paying a heavy price for the trial of *Lady Chatterley*. With the aid of hindsight, we can see that its upshot was the Great Train Robbery, the sixties, the Krays, Christine Keeler, Rachmanism, structuralism, taramasalata, Page 3, mushrooming massage parlours, rocketing venereal statistics and – most regrettably of all, perhaps – the collapse of Ealing Studios. 'Will the real Sir Guinness please step forward!' You had to laugh. (*See also* DE SANCHA, ANTONIA; KEELER, CHRISTINE; LAMBTON, LORD; *and* MELLOR, DAVID.)

Chaucer, Geoffrey: He was the father of English poetry, they say, yet he was no enemy of pleasure.

'He yaf neun the tavernes wel in evry toun/And kan nat stynte of syngyng by the weye.'

As my amusingly unpretentious friend 'Jeff' Bernard has pointed out, his cheery and loquacious pilgrims are as much a part of the English scene today as they were in the fourteenth century.

Nor, and correct me if I'm wrong, did he need an Arts Council grant of government subsidy to persuade him to his desk. Point made.

Geoffrey Chaucer: The E.O. Parrot of his day, the father of humorous versifying caught here in a reflective mood. It's a little known fact that as Secretary to Edward III, Chaucer founded the Inland Revenue and was its first Commissioner.

Were he alive today, he would, I think, be a stalwart of The Coach and Horses, Soho. Later being invited, no doubt, to become a Lord's Taverner and appear on *Desert Island Discs.* (*See also* ART, SUBSIDISED; *and* DRUNK, THE ENGLISH.)

Cheating: The true Englishman doesn't cheat. He might gain an edge, but that is an entirely different matter.

Unlike your little Pakistani cricketer, an Englishman doesn't tamper with the ball or, like your Australian, cast aspersions from the slips on the morals of the batsman's sister.

Crouched in the slips, Gooch and Gatting customarily discuss double-glazing and the price of sprouts. That said, an Englishman will aim the ball at the batsman's head or private parts – but that's in order. Cricket is a man's game and one below the belt is within the law – except that it isn't. However, if you don't like the kitchen, get out of the oven.

I was dissertating thus with the boy one day, when, to my surprise, he pointed out that Oxford usually cheat at sports.

'Surely not,' I said.

'Yes they do,' he said. 'Their rugger fifteen customarily includes three black line-backers, an Australian wrestler and four South Africans trained in Oriental fighting techniques. And take the Boat Race. When we went, their eight consisted of three Commonwealth gold medallists, four Yugoslav weightlifters and a Rhodes scholar who had rowed in the Olympics.'

'They were impostors,' I said. 'As you correctly observe, Oxford's once proud Boat Club has been hijacked – lock, stock and rowlock – by ambitious foreigners. The President is an Olympic oarsman from America and the coach a Pole. Felix Topolski, is it?'

'Small wonder they always win,' said the boy.

'They don't win,' I said. 'They cheat.'

I'd bested him yet again. (*See also* BOAT RACE, THE.)

Cheese, Beer and: I'd not in the general run of things promote the outmoded stuff of another travel writer here – least of all my friend Enoch Powell's *The Heart of England* – but glancing one evening through the book in the Malibu Bar of the Hyatt Hilton, Birmingham (I had business with the fat one with the cheque book), I was struck by some remarks there *in re* beer and cheese.

Having stumbled round Worcester for a while, inspecting tombs, ruins, cornices and so forth ('What queer tricks Dame Fate plays with men, so often preserving Squire Evil and destroying Mistress Good' – you'll get his drift), Powell repaired to a handy tavern.

'In an oak-panelled room,' he writes, 'where pewter glimmered like moonlight on still water, I poured a pint of ale down my throat. A comely, freckled maid, wearing a starched cap on her pretty little head, brought cheese on a plate, and a great paving-stone of bread.

'How, I wonder, have I refrained so long from praising bread, cheese and beer – the most significant, romantic, delicious, satisfying food that can pass the parched gullet of an English wayfarer! Men in saloon cars can nose through French menus for *sole colbert* and *Bordelaise,* and for many dishonest dishes devised by otherwise honest English cooks, but when I'm hungry and the white road lies behind me mile on weary mile, give me bread, cheese and beer.'

This is well said, I'll grant him that. I'm not a beer man myself –

preferring a sherry wine at six o'clock – but I am on all fours with Powell for once in the matter of *sole colbert* and *Bordelaise*. (*See also* BATH.)

Cinque Ports, The: A word to the wise. Thursday is the only day of the week on which Walmer Castle, in Kent, the residence of the Lord Warden of the *Cinque Ports*, is open to the public. We were fortunate. We pitched up on Friday, and were thus spared a conducted tour.

The Cinque Ports: The Duke of Wellington, England's greatest captain in the field, who gave his name to a boot. The Iron Duke knew better than anyone that to respect others you must first respect yourself. Thus, he never appeared in battle less than immaculately attired – the frock-coat fitting like a glove, the top hat polished, the cravat in place – as here at Waterloo. Once he had confounded Bonaparte, the little Corsican, politics became the Iron Duke's battlefield, but his sartorial standards never slipped. There might be a lesson here for such as the former Lord Stansgate, who is wont to address the House in a brown suit and common shoes.

That said, we were not spared two anecdotes discovered by Mrs Root in a picture-book – *The Captains and the Kings* by Sir Gummer, the little theologian – on sale in the vestibule. It seems that the Duke of Wellington, who died here in 1852, made no concessions to old age. With the whole of Walmer Castle to live in, he preferred one small bedroom modelled on a subaltern's tent. Here the victor of Waterloo slept on a horsehair pillow in an iron bed just three feet wide, and the only other article of furniture was a simple desk at which he wrote his letters standing up.

'Thank you, Mrs Root,' I said. 'Anything left of the pork pie?'

'According to Sir Gummer,' said Mrs Root, 'this grand old Tory, who resisted every reform with the stern formality of his native century, the eighteenth, remained a hero all his life, with one brief exception. When he opposed the Reform Bill, he rode slowly through London, high nosed and bleak of aspect, to the jeers of the mob and to a hail of brickbats and mud. As he reached Apsley House in Piccadilly, he said to the police constable at his side, "An odd day for them to choose." He had remembered that it was the anniversary of Waterloo.'

'We're obliged to you, Mrs Root,' I said. 'Is that it?'

'Not quite,' she said. 'Sir Gummer goes on to say that as he grew older the Duke's role merged naturally from that of Achilles into that of Nestor. He was consulted about everything. When the Crystal Palace was first erected in Hyde Park, the London sparrows failed to show proper respect for the assembled works of art and, with so much glass about, it was impossible to shoot them. So Queen Victoria sent for the Duke. The Duke would know what to do.

' "Sparrowhawks, Ma'am," he said immediately. "It was Wellington's last victory," comments Sir Gummer at the end.'

The anecdote had, after all, been worth the telling. Where but in England could a great conqueror's final victory have been over the humble London sparrow? (*See also* NELSON, ADMIRAL HORATIO; *and* QUEBEC HOUSE.)

Clowning: It is a sign of the times, perhaps, that clowning, as an hereditary profession, is dying out. Were it not, Mr Major might even now be residing in a circus caravan rather than at No. 10. Worse, in big tops throughout the land the English clown is being replaced by the French *auguste*.

Time was when the English clown, with bucket of water and attendant dwarf, could set kiddies on a roar from Land's End to

Clowning: He who laughs at a clown laughs at his own predicament. It is a sign of our sad national decline, surely, that Coco, the celebrated English clown – seen here (*above*) with big top colleagues, Charlie Dawkins and Corky Matthews, the bowler-hatted dwarf – has been replaced by the French *auguste* (*left*).

John o' Gaunt, but these days the French *auguste*, who wears a white hat fashioned in the manner of a traffic cone and plays the saxophone, prevails.

That said, we owe the following perception to Clive James, who is both Grock and Socrates, of course.

'Clowns are the poets of humour, wits its engineers. I myself can uniquely appear to prime-time advantage wearing either hat.'

Coaching: Are we in danger of coaching the natural talent out of our lads? It's the age-old argument: flair versus perseverence; artistry versus character; the little Continental playmaker against the English workhorse.

I know which side I'm on. Commentators may marvel briefly at 'the amazing natural talent of the little Jamaican who learned his cricket on a beach, playing with a banana and a coconut, and had never touched a bat until he was picked at the age of seventeen to play for the West Indies against Australia;' or equally, may remind us that 'Pele learned his ball skills heading an orange against a wall and had never set eyes on a football before scoring a hat trick in the World Cup of 1958.'

That's not our way. The English game is all about character and application – whether it's our cricketers, crouched heavily in the slips and looking more like the European butter mountain than natural atheletes, or a crew-cut Geordie booting a nippy little Continental winger into the five-pound seats.

These thoughts were prompted when I found myself with Mrs Root one day taking a sherry wine in the saloon bar of the Surveyor's Arms in Staines. The television set behind the bar happened to be showing a football match, so I expatiated for Mrs Root by reference to a little Italian youth who happened to be enjoying a lager two stools down.

'Isn't that right, Benito?' I said. 'You'll have learned your ball skills, such as they are, by kicking a melon around the streets of Naples. Not your fault, if, on arriving here to open a pizza bar in Staines, you found yourself up-ended on the park by English character and application.'

'Actually,' said Benito, 'I was born in Streatham.'

'In that case,' I said, 'you'll have noticed that we ourselves (I'm referring here not to your sort, but to indigenous lads with flat-top hairstyles) are not without our skilful players: lads who can put their foot on the ball, slow the game down and examine their options. Take the lad, Gazza. As daft as a brush, but all the skill in the world.'

It was my bad luck that at that point clips came up on the TV screen of the 1991 Cup Final – not least one of Gazza scything at an opponent's ankles, landing on his arse and breaking his leg in eighteen places.

'Good gracious me,' said Benito. 'That didn't look very skilful.'

'My point holds none the less,' I said. 'How are you settling in?' (*See also* AMATEUR, THE GIFTED.)

Debutantes: Time was when debutantes came out. Now it's so-called gays. Were a proud father and his consort to announce in tomorrow's *Daily Telegraph* that their daughter Caroline was coming out, we'd take their drift to be that she'd joined a crew of crop-haired Sapphists to present lunchtime theatre in a garage, plus and further that her 'significant other' was a lady in building-site boots.

The season, was it? Plump girls 'finished' by Constance Spry as was – presented to Her Majesty on a lawn? I'll say this for the season.

Debutantes: Had Her Majesty not ill-advisedly discontinued the very English practice of the 'Season', younger members of her court might have had better things to do than appear topless in the tabloids, locked uncompromisingly with those beneath them. Here, debutantes line up on the stairs to have their bloodstock potential judged — the bosom, the hips, the upper thigh — before being whisked off to stud in Gloucestershire.

Had it obtained in my daughter Doreen's day, I'd have had her do it. 'Nice place you've got here, Your Majesty. This is my daughter Doreen. Don't laugh.' That would have knocked the sociology out of her.

In fact I blame the demise of the season for much which has gone wrong *in re* the younger Royals, and I said as much one day to Partridge.

'Instead of doing the season,' I said, 'the Ferguson woman became a chalet girl, cavorting in Switzerland. *Après ski* with such as Paddy MacNally, the little motor mechanic. Had she and the Princess of Wales done the season – firing champagne corks from Knightsbridge balconies at the lower orders trudging home from work – they'd have got all that out of their systems before marrying up. They'd not subsequently have concealed Sony Walkmans under their hairstyles and tapped their feet to so-called Spandau Ballet during the one minute's silence at the cenotaph. Nor would they have snow-wrestled one another *après ski*. Most to the point, they'd not have bolted.'

I got an argument, of course. 'But Mr Root,' the boy said, 'their mothers came out and they bolted quick enough. Diana's mother ran off to Scotland with a cattle breeder and Fergie's mother eloped with an Argentine polo player.'

'And so would you have done,' I said, 'had you landed up with "Johnnie" Spencer or, worse, my friend Major "Ronnie" Ferguson.'

The boy came in at a different angle, hoping, no doubt, to catch me unawares.

'What about Lady "Melons" Windsor?' he said.

He had me there. I played for time. 'The jury's out on Lady "Melons" Windsor,' I said.

'My point is that *her* mother didn't bolt.'

'She may not have done,' I said, 'but Lady "Melons" Windsor didn't come out.'

'Nor has Prince Edward,' said the boy.

What was he on about? 'My point precisely,' I said.

I'd confounded him yet again. (*See also* BLANDFORD, THE MARQUESS OF.)

Denning, Lord: A great jurist and, more importantly, a great Englishman, of whom it could properly be said that he was the champion of our ancient liberties and institutions – such as the citizen's right to be tried by an all-white jury, not least if he himself is black. (*See also* JURY-RIGGING.)

As Master of the Rolls, he ruled (The Collector of Taxes versus Rossminster & Accomplices, 1979) that an Englishman's castle is his home – a judgement which my next-door neighbour, Alderman Entwistle (rtd) would do well to heed. Plus, in another important case, he appeared as himself in the matter of a footpath before the Hampshire bench, thus refuting the old adage that a lawyer who represents himself has an ass as a client. Or he would have refuted it had he won.

Lord Denning: At the age of ninety-four, Lord Denning still hands down judgements – 'If a chap's in prison he must be a felon. Common sense, I'd have thought' – which have lost none of their power to cut through cant and sentimental waffle.

Some say he later lost his marbles. At the age of ninety, he was still handing down judgements in language which a six-year-old could understand, though not, alas, the House of Lords. Lord Hailsham, sitting on the Stone of Scone, overturned seventy-eight per cent of Denning's later judgements, and many were shocked when he went the other way *in re* the matter of the Guildford Four.

It would have been better, said Denning, had capital punishment still obtained. The Guildford Four would have been hanged and the matter closed. What, argued Denning, were four lives compared to the reputation of British justice? *In pro bono publico* and so forth. In fact, I'd not go along with this, and researching the Inns of Court one day I said as much to the boy.

'It may surprise you to know,' I said, 'that I am not currently in favour of the gibbet, having been persuaded thus by my Esher neighbour, Sir Robert Mark, as was. Sir Mark is an unashamed non-hanger, not because capital punishment is morally objectionable but because on balance it doesn't work. "Since mistakes can occur," reasons Sir Mark, "why hand liberals a stick to beat us with?" A knockdown argument, I think you'll concede.'

'Indeed,' said the boy. 'Keeping a man in prison for the rest of his life for something he didn't do is one thing; hanging him is all too likely to elicit a shrill cry of protest from the compassion industry.'

The boy persists in thinking that I can't spot irony. In the general run of things I'd have clipped him round the ear, but taking heed of our whereabouts and the current way of doing things – a Scotsman on the Stone of Scone; a Lord Chief Justice who plays the piano, appears without his wig and has a 'media adviser'; a leader of the Temple, who wears suede shoes and combs his hair in public (Scrivener, is it?) – I refuted him instead in his own terms.

'In fact,' I said, 'life for something you didn't do would be a little steep. Fifteen years would be enough.'

Then I clipped him round the ear. (*See also* GIBBET, THE; *and* JUSTICE, BRITISH.)

De Sancha, Antonia: I'll not comment on so-called Antonia de Sancha and David Mellor, our respected ex-Minister for Heritage and so forth. I'll not add further to the distress of his blameless wife and children by rehearsing the lewd facts again. That's not my way.

I'll leave that to the media hypocrites of the tabloid press, armed with strobe, ladder and telephoto lens.

I'll not remind his children over breakfast that a little foreign 'actress' – attired in a basque in the early afternoon – lured their father to her West Kensington boudoir, thereafter entrapping him there again and again.

That's not my way. I will say this, however. Mellor's ordeal has

Antonia de Sancha: Max Clifford, the little publicist – here attending a tea-dance with Antonia de Sancha, the foreign 'model' – keeps a firm grip on his client's arm. Were he to let go, she'd unzip her dress, don a *basque* and seek to compromise a blameless Tory politician.

been a timely reminder to those of us in the public eye that we can never for a moment drop our guard. With the lowering of frontiers – and a woman in charge at VAT and Excise – stiletto-legged 'actresses' (their strings pulled by a PR supremo and versed in techniques acquired on the Continent) could entrap an Englishman even as he discussed the merits of competing firebricks at an Esher barbecue. (*See also* KEELER, CHRISTINE; LAMBTON, LORD; *and* MELLOR, DAVID.)

Devlin, Lord: Another great, and essentially English, jurist, to whom we owe the concept of 'The Man on the Clapham Omnibus' – positing this commonsensical Englishman against ivory tower academics such as Professor Dworkin, an American, needless to say – of Oxford.

So-called Dworkin wants to separate law and morality (a typically head-in-the-clouds notion for which, as the *Daily Telegraph* has perceived, we are now paying a heavy price in terms of damage to our property). But Devlin held that it was the business of the law to intrude into private matters – basques, indecency and so forth – rulings as to what was right and wrong being what the Man on the Clapham Omnibus felt in his water to be so.

Judging it appertaining that we should put some flesh on this ghostly frame, I told the boy that I'd wire him for sound one day and take him for a trip, not on the Clapham Omnibus – since no such thing was currently extant – but on a 137 bus trading between Sloane Square and Brixton. By dint of quizzing on the top deck – 'Speak up, madam, we represent Central Television' – we'd learn, I said, what ordinary, decent Londoners believe in their water to be true. (*See also* OMNIBUS, THE CLAPHAM.)

Drake, Sir Francis: On the way to Land's End, we stop off in Plymouth to honour Drake, and what do we get from the boy? A wedge of harmonised history as per EEC Directive BFC56789D, and of the sort which my friend Booker derides each week in the *Sunday Telegraph*.

' "He clapped his glass to his sightless eye and 'I'm damned if I see it,' he said" as Newbolt, the patriotic versifier, had it. They don't write them like that any more.'

'That was Nelson,' said the boy.

'I dare say it was,' I said. 'However, the point I'm making is that in those days an Englishman had his priorities right: he wasn't to be diverted from his game of bowls by a few thousand Spanish men of war sailing up the Channel. "You have heard of the beat of the off-shore wind/And the thresh of the deep sea rain." Newbolt again, I think.'

'Kipling, in fact,' said the boy. 'And in any case, the Armada would never have set sail had not Drake unpardonably provoked the Spanish by pillaging their property in the Caribbean. He was a pirate, Mr Root, an extortioner, a drunken hooligan, who, in any case, didn't defeat the Armada. As every schoolboy now knows, it was sunk by a sudden squall.'

I'd heard enough. 'He may have been a pirate,' I said, 'but he singed a beard or two in his time. Cadiz, was it? We could do with a few hooligans of his sort now.'

Sitting outside an agreeable olde tavern on Plymouth Hoe, we were approached at this moment by two local youths who said that they would refrain from spitting in our lagers if I gave them twenty pounds.

Drake, Sir Francis: Remembered mainly as our greatest sea-dog, Sir Drake in fact was something of a politician. As MP for Bossiney in Devon, he anticipated the Enterprise Culture, advising his constituents to stand on their own two feet and help themselves – his own policy with regard to Spanish gold.

Had I been alone, I'd have dispersed them with a rolled-up copy of the *Daily Telegraph*, but, careful for the safety of the boy and Mrs Root, I handed over the money – whereupon they spat in our beer in any case.

'Nothing wrong with that,' said the boy. 'Merely the spirit of Merrie England.'

'Precisely,' I said. He's catching on. (*See also* NELSON, ADMIRAL HORATIO.)

Dramatics, Amateur: It is an agreeable, and healthy, irony, that we English, who don't notably support the arts, excel at pageants and amateur dramatics.

Few market towns are without their local Musical Comedy Society – the Midland Bank's production of *West Side Story*, with the manager's lady and a one-legged teller as the doomed lovers, Maria from Costa Rica and the other one, being a particular favourite. Nor is there any abatement in the provinces of processions, floats and so forth –

the butcher's wife as Lady Godiva, the *garagiste* as Peeping Tom – marking historical occurrences.

An encouraging indication that we in Merrie England can still make our own entertainment. That said, I'd rather watch Anne Diamond filling a settee on breakfast television or Anneka Rice, the little Swede.

Amateur Dramatics: Merrie England survives in Romford. In spite of competition from theme pubs and satellite erotica, there's a good turn-out to cheer these fat ladies on a float: the sub-postmistress as the Queen of May, members of the PTA as her attendant sylphs. Truly, we English lead the world in pageantry.

Drunk, The English: He enjoys an honoured place in our literature and history.

Alas, the new spirit of puritanism which stalks the land has decreed that the Old Bill, instead of prosecuting villains, should persecute the law-abiding middle classes, setting up road blocks and breath-testing gentlemen *littérateurs* as they drive on the wrong side of the road through Somerset. Were Falstaff alive today, he'd be breathalised on his way to take tea with Hal at Windsor.

Expositing thus for the boy one day as we drove to Dover – there to check on the little woman in charge of VAT and Excise – I was interrupted as usual by a volley of specious 'statistics'.

'As it happens, Mr Root,' he said, 'it is widely recognised by doctors, psychiatrists and senior policemen that alcohol is the greatest social menace presently afflicting the country. Britain now has more than a million alcoholics. An article in the *Independent* on 5th June 1992 revealed that alcohol is linked with half the road deaths involving young people, eighty per cent of deaths from fire, fifty per cent of murders, sixty-six per cent of attempted suicides and thirty-three per cent of accidents in the home. It also plays a part in at least one in three marital break-ups.'

He'd played into my hands. 'For one thing,' I said, 'you can prove anything with statistics. For another, you don't want to believe what you read in the *Independent*. You'll be on drugs, I take it? Cannabis, is it?'

The boy hadn't had enough. 'I'm afraid you're a little out of date, Mr Root,' he said. 'That's a very sixties concept, if I may say so. These days, young people prefer to keep a clear head. That said, alcohol is as much a drug, of course, as any other.'

Here we go, I thought. The boy was inferring that there was no distinction between my good self after a sherry wine and a crack-crazed Rastafarian coming through my privet hedge to drop excreta down my chimney-pot. There'd be statistics to follow, unless I was much mistaken.

'Not that that's any argument for prohibition,' the boy continued. 'Indeed, the latest evidence from Amsterdam suggests that all drugs should be legalised as a matter of urgency. Liberal policies in Holland have resulted in a marked decrease in addiction, in drug-related crime and in the spread of the HIV virus.'

I ask you. Happily, I had a world-class argument up my sleeve. 'If Amsterdam is such a paradise on earth,' I said. 'Why don't you go and live there? Anything left of the pork pie, Mrs Root?'

The boy was lost for words, of course, unable to continue with this black-belt intellectual discourse.

Arrived at Dover, I presented myself at various checkpoints, introduced myself under an alias to test the system. I'd not want them to know I was a media figure. Egon Ronay, of the famous guide, never checks a restaurant as himself.

'Alderman Entwistle of Esher,' I said. 'Here to check our frontiers with the little woman in charge of VAT and Excise. I wish to ascertain that those of ethnic derivation are getting the full strip-search. Plus, I'd search the boy if I were you. He isn't ethnic, but my guess is he's carrying drugs.'

The system works – after a fashion. The boy was ignored, but they strip-searched me – the upshot of a call to Esher which established that Entwistle hadn't paid his Poll Tax.

Every cloud etc. I was held in a room for problematic visitors, later charged with the minor misdemeanour of assuming a false identity. A small price to pay for the deliverance of Entwistle into my hands. I'd make him the laughing stock of Esher, issue lampoons *in re* aldermen who duck their taxes.

That was the up-side of our visit. The down-side was the discovery that the little woman in charge of VAT and Excise trades in London. How can she monitor from there the influx of abstract ideas, rabies and trans-Continental drug fiends at our Channel ports? I'd have a word with her in London. (*See also* AMSTERDAM, THE LATEST EVIDENCE FROM; ENTWISTLE, ALDERMAN; FALSTAFF, JACK; *and* FRONTIERS, OUR.)

Education: The debate continues. In my day it was the three 'R's and a clip round the ear. The upshot? Half the sixth form was on parole, the masters likewise. Nothing wrong with that.

Nor was I taught so-called harmonised history, as per the boy. (*See* DRAKE, SIR FRANCIS.) I wasn't taught anything, in fact, since I left school at fourteen, took over my grandfather's whelk stall at the business end of a writ, and continued with my further education at the University of Real Life.

Education: I've heard it said that my friend Lord Chingford isn't as nice as he looks, but I'd not concur. A pub forecourt philosopher like myself, Chingford boasts that he never passed an exam in his life. So much for education!

Which is why I'm more than able to see the boy off in any intellectual discourse. He has had the misfortune to have been 'educated'
under the modern way of doing things – as per Dame Williams, the
little Social Democrat. We know what that means. Pop music in class,
the cane and buckled belt eschewed, discipline up the Swannee and
pupils marking their own exam papers, since such is deemed better
than that some should be seen as cleverer than others.

That said, and to discover whether standards still prevail in the
private sector – fagging, bullying, boys lashed to a whipping block
for the good of their souls etc – I ruled that we'd visit a public school.

'We'll visit Eton,' I said. 'Two birds with one stone, since we'll
drop in at Windsor Castle too – check on whether the latter has
been restored to Her Majesty's pleasure and at our expense. Have
you anything to say, young Partridge?'

I'd been expecting some weasel words *in re* Joe Public having to
pay for the restoration of Her Majesty's common parts and Canalettos,
but he held his peace. The boy's learning. The occasional clip round
the ear has had an effect. (*See also* BULLYING; *and* ETON.)

Education, The Uselessness of Higher: If the boy's an example,

you can keep it. Come to that, you can keep my daughter Doreen
too. Doreen, as I've said before, I think, studied so-called Sociology at
a polytechnic, thereafter attended a teacher training college for eight
years, got a job teaching Compassion and Statistics in a day-school
and was made redundant two weeks later.

I had to laugh, was still laughing when she came to live at
home. I stopped laughing, however, when, on her first day, she
tried to participate gratis in the evening meal.

'That will be five pounds and seventy-five pence,' I said. 'Coffee
extra.'

Mrs Root was quite shocked. 'That's very hard, Henry!' she said.
'Doreen's unemployed.'

'There are three million unemployed,' I said, 'but they don't all
come here and eat my fish pie.'

Alas, when considering further education for the girl, I'd not
had Sam Johnson's adage up my sleeve.

'A man in general,' Sam said, 'is better pleased when he has a
good dinner than when his wife has Greek.'

Had he said 'Sociology' he'd have hit the nail on the head. Meanwhile, the girl's still with us and shows no signs of leaving. I've
now got two politically correct young folk on my hands. All I need

is for Henry Junior to pitch up suddenly from Amsterdam, where, I gather, he's dancing on a pedestal in feathers.

'If Henry Junior rings,' I said to Mrs Root, 'tell him we've moved.'

Efficiency, Business: The debate continues as to whether business efficiency as such is an English concept. Some prefer nonchalance in the boardroom, deeming efficiency as being more appropriate to Japs and Germans. (*See also* AMATEUR, THE GIFTED.)

For myself, I'm in two minds. In building up Henry Root Wet Fish, my own method was to drive by the seat of my pants, to stand up close and use the knuckle rather than deploy book-keepers and cost-watching analysts. The bottom line was in my head: my competitors laid out cold like dead mackerel on their slabs.

On the other hand, if you wish to participate in what *is* an English concept – I refer to privilege in general, the honours system in particular – visible profits are of the essence.

And here's my problem. Since I retired from the day-to-day management of Henry Root Wet Fish, it has not been performing to capacity under its new directors. It jogs along. My dividends are adequate, but it's not the cash cow it was in my day, and a cash cow is what you need if you're of a mind to 'buy' an honour from the Tories.

The matter became fully focused in my mind when, during a break in our research re 'Merrie England – Whither?', I sat down with the *Daily Telegraph* one day to peruse therein Her Majesty's Birthday Honours List.

'Goats and monkeys, Mrs Root!' I said. 'What a crew! Ballet dancers, hurdlers, jacks-in-office! I could have one of these. A knighthood at least, a seat in the Lords at best.'

Having calculated that the going rate under the Tories might be in excess of half a million pounds, I quickly realised that such would not be forthcoming from Henry Root Wet Fish under its new directors.

'A troubleshooter, that's what's needed, Mrs Root,' I said. 'An asset-stripper with axe and calculator to turn the business round. Who's the large one with an excess of facial hair who troubleshoots for England? Arrives when least expected with camera crew in tow? Sir Harvey-Jones, is that it? I'm of a mind to call him in.'

I later pitched up at Sir Jones's office, in no time had him dancing to my tune.

'Peas in a pod, you and I, Sir Jones,' I said. 'You turn my

Sir Edward Elgar: His style differed from that of Sir Lloyd Webber, seen here leaving the theatre with Sarah Brightman, the little soprano. We may be thankful that Sir Webber's musical arrangements — the big, ballooning ballads with a patriotic underthump — are more characteristically English than the arrangements appertaining to his private life. Shortly after this picture was taken, Miss Brightman was written out of the score, her place being taken by the third Lady Webber in a more suitable skirt. Old Vaughan Williams and Sir Britten must be turning in their graves.

business round and, as a *quid pro quo*, I'll guarantee your head appears in *Root Around Britain* next to mine. How much, by the way, did you lob the Tories *in re* yours? We're off the record here.'

He chuckled deeply, tapped his nose, then tried to negotiate with regard to billing, residuals and so forth – even suggested that the title might be changed to *Root and Sir Jones Around Britain*. I maintained a poker player's mien, made vague promises in the knowledge that in the media game these are quickly broken, that many's the clever negotiator who's ended up on the cutting-room floor.

A deal was struck, a rendezvous made in two weeks' time. On that occasion, Sir Jones and I would visit the offices of Henry Root Wet Fish Ltd, Billingsgate, where he'd carry out a preliminary investigation.

I'll not prejudge the issue, but I will say this: were I Mortimer, my successor in the chair, I'd already feel the axe whistling above my neck. (*See also* FISHMONGER, A SIMPLE; HARVEY-JONES, SIR JOHN; *and* HONOURS.)

Elgar, Sir Edward: 'Pomp and Circumstance', is it? The last night of the Proms? Weedy young men in British Bulldog toppers? Fat girls in specs carrying patriotic mascots? A tipsy conductor trying to be funny? 'Rule Britannia' as an encore? It's reassuring to discover that such essentially English scenes survive.

Born into a musical household, Sir Elgar was a man of considerable urbanity, I'm told, often cutting an orchestral rehearsal short in time for the first race at Kempton Park. You'd not have found Sibelius, the gloomy Swede, cutting a rehearsal short, I'll wager, to attend a horse race, nor Paderewski, the long-haired Pole.

Nor, I may say, was it Sir Elgar's habit to pitch up at Kempton Park with a soprano on his arm. Times change. Much as I admire Sir Lloyd Webber, the balloon-faced cellist, were he to be seen at Kempton Park, it would be odds on he'd have a little soprano on his arm. Sir Webber trades up in little sopranos as if they were going out of fashion. Sir Elgar wouldn't have been seen at Kempton Park with other than Lady Elgar on his arm. So much for English music.

Elizabeth I (left) and Baroness Finchley (right): The most English of monarchs, Elizabeth gave her name to an age, just as Baroness Thatcher (seen here disguised as a cabbage while she spies on social security scroungers) gave her name to a decade. It is too easily forgotten that we English have always been at our best with our backs to the wall and a woman against the helm.

Entwistle, Alderman: To be a small fish in a small pond is one thing – and bad enough. To be remembered merely as a passing footnote in another man's reference book – and this for not having paid your Poll Tax! – is quite another.

Still, Entwistle brought it upon himself. Had he not tried to thwart me in the matter of permissions for my erection, the world would not have heard of him merely as a little Hitler and local jack-in-office; it would not have heard of him at all.

Meanwhile, my campaign of vilification is under way. Posters have been put up in Esher and pamphlets distributed, announcing that this petty bureaucrat is in arrears. (*See also* ENTWISTLE, THE WRONG; *and* SHAKESPEARE AND SHAKESPEARE.)

Entwistle, The Wrong: My mistake – albeit a trivial one. It seems I've vilified the wrong man. It so transpires that the Entwistle who hasn't paid his Poll Tax is not the vexatious jack-in-office but a local *garagiste* of the same initial who also resides in Esher. I blame the little functionary in Dover whom I furnished with an alias. He should have checked more carefully.

Meanwhile, the right Entwistle has issued a blizzard of lawyer's letters, injunctions and gagging orders against my good self of the other part. Indeed, Harbottle & Lewis, representing Entwistle, and trading in Bruton Street, W1, inform me that unless I discontinue pronto with my slanders I'll be up for contempt of court before the local beak!

The girl Doreen's come up trumps for once, urging me not to give ground to these local bureaucrats or their smart West End representatives.

'It's the system, Daddy,' she said, 'trying to grind you down. You're a small man who . . .'

I wasn't having that. 'Do what?' I said. 'I'm not a small man, and I'd thank you to mind your tongue, my girl.'

'I was talking politically,' she said. 'This is a *political* issue, don't you see? They're trying to deny you freedom of speech. You *must* fight on.'

She was right about that and no mistake. An Englishman will not be gagged. Entwistle may well have paid his Poll Tax but I'll call him a horse notwithstanding. (*See also* MAN, THE SMALL; *and* SHAKESPEARE AND SHAKESPEARE.)

Eton: A fruitful day out. Down to Windsor with the boy and Mrs Root, where I seconded Mrs Root to cover English Heritage ('Once round the castle, Mrs Root, that should do it, and if you see Her Majesty, don't mention the Ferguson woman if you want to stay to tea') while the boy and I researched the school.

'This is more like it,' I said, as we paced the ivy-covered quads. 'With luck we'll see a junior flogged on Sexton's Piece. Arse up over a whipping block, a proctor in topper holding either arm. We'll call on the Head in chambers.'

We banged around a bit, dropped in on classes ('Geography, is it? Carry on'), marked parents' cards ('Don't worry about the floggings – simple tradition, nothing more'), eventually ran the Head to earth in his own front room.

'Henry Root,' I said. 'Researching all aspects of the school for Central Television. We hope to find that bullying still obtains. Toasted in front of a fire and so forth. Nothing wrong with that. Untoasted, how is a lad, in later life, to become a major playwright?'

The Head, though clearly glad to see me, adopted a cautious

stance, as many do when confronted by the prospect of peak-time exposure in our lounge-rooms.

'Bullying, Mr Root?' he said. 'That's very much a thing of the past, I'm glad to say. We certainly don't countenance anything like that.'

'Of course, of course,' I said, at the same time winking at the boy, and apprising him *sotto voce* that we had one here. 'That's what they all say,' I whispered to the boy. 'You're running the tape machine, I hope?'

Eton: Town and topper. Watched cheerfully by three local oiks, a brace of Eton new boys wait at Windsor Station for a taxi which will take them to tea and toasted crumpets with Mr and Mrs M'Tutor at their 'House'. The oiks' unenvious demeanour is a timely refutation of the attempts, by mean-minded egalitarians in the media, to whip up class hatred in Mr Major's Britain.

'Times have changed, Mr Root,' the Head continued. 'We concentrate now on academic excellence. We can't compete with Winchester, of course, but we do pride ourselves on the number of our pupils who go on to university. That's the point I'd wish to make if I appeared on your television programme.'

'With due respect, Headmaster,' I said, 'I'll be the judge of what makes peak-time viewing, and you won't mind my saying that it's not stuff *in re* academic excellence. We're not talking BBC 2 here. We're talking prime-time slots. We could be up against Jeremy Beadle or the fat Australian. We'll need a flogging if we're to beat Beadle in the ratings.'

The Head continued to resist; more accurately, played for time. ' "Time's winged chariot . . ." Mr Root,' he said. 'I'm afraid you'll have to excuse me now. I have to make preparations for Agar's Feast.'

'Agar's Feast? What's that?' I said.

'It's a school ceremony which has been held on Foundation Day for several hundred years. Dinner is held in Agar's Hall, the Board of Governors attend and the Provost gives the address in Latin. Boys who are about to leave are reminded of the school's traditions.'

That was more like it. The school's traditions, eh? We knew what they were. Ritual, sodomy and privilege. I'd attend the do with camera crew and strobe. We could beat the fat Australian with this one.

'We'll be off now,' I said. 'See you at Agar's Feast.'

The Headmaster started to demur, was caught up in an interior struggle, clearly, between the need to protect the school's voodoo ceremonies from prying eyes and his natural desire to prevail against the fat Australian in a prime-time slot.

'I'm not really sure, Mr Root . . .' he said.

'Please, Headmaster,' I said. 'I'll be the judge as to what's best for the reputation of the school. See you at Agar's Feast. When is it, by the way?'

'July 18th,' he said. 'But I really think . . .'

'See you on the 18th,' I said.

We then returned to Esher, at which point I realised that we'd left Mrs Root at Windsor Castle. She got back eventually by train, and seemed in excellent spirits.

'I was utterly *enthralled*, Henry,' she said. 'The Castle's a veritable depository of our history.'

'Never mind that, Mrs Root,' I said. 'I'm waiting for my supper.'

(*See also* FEAST, AGAR'S.)

Failure, A: As if the boy Partridge weren't excess baggage enough, my research on *Root Around Britain* is not much helped by the constant, carping presence of my politically correct, heavily subsidised daughter, Doreen, who is still my lodger and shows no sign of leaving.

When over breakfast, I observed, pleasantly enough, that she should seek employment of some sort, since endemic failure was bad for the character, I received a right-on – you'll forgive the parlance – burst.

'Oh dear,' she said, laying down her *Guardian* and assuming an expression of pained forebearance as if addressing the village idiot. 'Failure, surely is one of those big words, like "freedom" or "democracy", whose interpretation is entirely relative.'

The boy, who, I admit, sometimes serves his purpose, wasn't present and I was temporarily unable to recall details of Professor Williams *in re* the relativist fallacy. I therefore played for time.

'I'm merely saying,' I said, 'that someone who has been trained for eleven years at the taxpayers' expense and is then unable to find employment could be counted in some sense as a failure.'

The girl snorted contemptuously. 'A person who has "failed" in the marketplace of life,' she said, 'often perceives things that a so-called "successful" person would have been too preoccupied to notice. Equally, what you choose to call a "failure" could be described as a successful person who refused to be herded along convenient lines by the ruling class.'

I wasn't having that. 'I beg to differ,' I said. 'I don't have a chain of wet fish outlets, three cars in the garage and a musical cocktail cabinet fashioned, like Michael Parkinson's, in the manner of Hercules holding up the globe, because I was herded along convenient lines. I may veer to the conventional and orthodox in my modes and habits, but I *worked* for my success.'

'*Success*!?!' she cried. 'You're a fishmonger, Daddy!'

I was speechless, frankly, a state, I may say, to which I'd never been rendered by the boy. I'll say this for the girl: she's a chip off the old block. And she'll be looking very foolish when, thanks to Sir Jones's troubleshooting, I become Sir Root – Lord Root, even. In which latter case, the girl would become the Hon Doreen Root, unless I'm much mistaken. She'd not like that. (*See also* FISHMONGER, A SIMPLE.)

Falstaff, Jack: Often cited by my friend 'Dick' West as a great and quintessential Englishman – not least when expressing his own very manly preference for real ale, brewed in Norfolk, over bottled lager or your French Sancerre.

'What was good enough for Jack Falstaff is good enough for me!' proclaims West – and more than once – in his remaindered book, *An English Journey*.

Driving back to Esher after our trip to Eton – and taking the so-called Merry Wives of Windsor as my cue – I happened to mention this to the boy, whereupon he tried to ensnare me in the brittle web of a 'philosophical' conundrum.

'By an adroit variation on the "Ontological Argument",' he said, 'which, as you'll know, holds that God's perfection entails His existence, we could argue that no Englishman could reasonably be called great or quintessential who didn't actually exist. Falstaff was a fiction.'

I wasn't having that. 'He may have been a fiction,' I said, 'and a drunk and a whoremonger to boot – Mistress Pym, was it? And the Quickly woman? – but he came up trumps at Agincourt. Or was that Quince the Weaver? He was another. Don't tell me about drunks and whoremongers. Did you, by the way, hear about the dyslexic Irish pimp who bought a warehouse?'

An innocent, and very English, jest, I think you'll agree, but the boy looked as if he'd bitten on a lemon. I'd fallen foul, clearly, of the latest edict *in re* political correctness – not, I may say, without intention.

'I find that remark exceedingly offensive, Mr Root,' he said. 'It is both racist and an insult to a disadvantaged minority. Be that as it may, I think you may be confusing Falstaff and Quince the Weaver, as you call him, with Pistol. Pistol was at Agincourt, where, if you remember, Llewelyn obliged him as a braggart to eat a leek.'

Confounded by a Welshman? That seemed unlikely – though I refrained from saying so, rather than be judged politically incorrect again. Instead, I came in at a different angle.

'As usual, you miss my drift,' I said. 'I'd not aver that a great *fictional* Englishman would necessarily loom larger than the extant Welsh – druids, Men of Harlech, miners descanting self-pitying dirges down a pit and so forth – except that he would. I rest my case.'

The boy resorted to a sullen silence. I'd out-argued him yet again.

Feast, Agar's: Having decided to get this in the can while the iron was hot (the way things were going, such a patrician ritual might, in Major's England, be discontinued under Unacceptable Privilege etc.), I set about engaging sound, camera crew and *mise en scène.*

Not wishing to attend the ceremony too conspicuously, I had intended to restrict the crew to myself as *mise en scène,* backed up by one gym-shoed young operative on camera and another with appropriate recording gear.

All too predictably, the boy put up an argument, claiming that such would infringe union regulation 768397XDB *in re* minimum crews and so forth, insisting that we should saddle ourselves with sparks, first assistant, make-up girls and grip.

'A monkey in your pocket,' I said, 'to keep your mouth shut,' whereupon the boy's liberal principles were satisfied, of course, and off we went – Smithers, from *Root Into Europe*, with handheld video recorder, Midgely with boom and earphones, the boy, Partridge and, in order to blend, myself as *mise en scène,* attired in hired morning suit and Eton topper.

Arrived at Eton, we made our way to Agar's Hall and infiltrated ourselves incognito. 'Don't mind us,' I said. 'We represent Central Television. I fixed it with the Head. Carry on.'

And what a carry-on it was. Suffice it to say, I think, that such had not been in the can before – not anyway since the fat one with attendant camera crew (Roger Cook, is it?) stumbled unwittingly on sixteen High Court judges and their clerks carrying out a Masonic initiation rite on Hampstead Heath.

First, a melancholy procession into Agar's Feast, with school leavers carried shoulder high in candlelight on ceremonial silver plates. The Head then made a speech in Latin about leadership, privilege and standards. The President of Pop replied in Greek. Next up, the Senior Chaplain induced targeted boys into MI5, thereafter administering the school oath, anally. A one-legged Field Marshal led the Dame's Chorus of 'Abide With Me', followed by the Dance of the Tiny Tugs. Finally, to a mighty roar of *'Floreat Etona!'*, Agar's relics were lowered on a kebab skewer from the Minstrel's Gallery.

The ceremony over, emotional members of Pop French-kissed their fags, obsequious tradesmen from the town sought to collect on overdue accounts and were whipped off the premises. A departing Nigerian prince presented M'Tutor and Mrs M'Tutor with jewellery and other expensive gifts. I instructed the boy to capture this latter and very telling event on film.

'Jump to it!' I said. 'Get the black prince in frame.'

The boy assumed his *Guardian* reader's mien, and started to demur. 'I'll not be a party,' he said, 'to patronising a token black.'

I had his number. 'There'll be a BAFTA in it,' I said. 'Yourself in pumps presented with a statue by the Princess Royal . . .'

The boy sprang into action.

'Over here, Winston!' he cried. 'As quick as you like!'

I was thinking how privileged we were to be at such a typically English scene, when a Bulldog or somesuch grabbed each of my operatives by the collar and attempted to ejaculate them, having first challenged me as to who they and I might be.

'They're not with me,' I said. 'As you can see from my attire, I'm a Fellow of this establishment, standing in for old Lord Home who, alas, is incommoded.'

The police were called, my crew arrested for infiltration, and I returned to Esher, satisfied with a job well done. It would do the boy no harm to spend the night as a guest of the constabulary. He'd learn something of the risks a docudramatist must take if he wishes to get pertinent matters in the can. (*See also* ETON.)

Fishmonger, A Simple: A fishmonger, was I? I'd not been called that before; not until the girl thus posited me over breakfast. That's not how I'd seen myself. I'd seen myself as a high-street entrepreneur, and as such eligible for an honour – as per Lord Wolfson, the little draper; Lord Clore, the shoe salesman; and Lord Sainsbury, the high-street grocer.

That said, Lord Root the fishmonger didn't – as I now saw – have the desired resonance. I therefore decided that Sir Jones the troubleshooter's job would be to strip the assets of Henry Root Wet Fish, fire personnel and liquidate the properties – thus yielding sufficient cash with which to buy an honour from the Tories and allow me to designate myself as Lord Root the financier, an entrepreneur of the old school whose wealth had been mysteriously, but appropriately, acquired.

'Quite frankly, Mrs Root,' I said, 'we look like yuppies, you and I. We smack of retail. In future, I'll deny my links with fish. There must be an aroma of old money at every turn. I'll dress down. Acquire some ancestral trousers from a sale. You'll be all right. They'll not meet you.'

Later, on the way to the offices of Henry Root Wet Fish with Sir Jones, I thus instructed him. 'Wield the axe ruthlessly, Sir Jones,' I said. 'Let not your hand be stayed by sentiment. A gong's what I'm after, so cash is of the essence – as you'll know yourself. How *did* you get yours, by the way? Never mind – nod's as good as a wink and so forth.'

Later, as I showed him round the business, I tipped him off – without officiously pre-empting him, I think – as to where the axe should fall.

'This is our Managing Director, Mortimer,' I said. 'A word in your ear, Sir Jones. He'll have to go. Wedded to the old ways, keen to retain our links with fish. And this is Froggart, who, man and boy, has toiled here for fifty years. He knows more about how to pack a haddock than you could learn in a month of Sundays but he's ready for the scrapheap. Just marking your card.'

I could see that Sir Jones was impressed by my assessments, rummaged around, went through books and so forth. Finally said that the axe would fall where appropriate on Tuesday week. I can hardly wait. I'd not be in Mortimer's shoes, or Froggart's either, come to that. (*See also* HARVEY-JONES, SIR JOHN; *and* HONOURS.)

Flanders, The Mud of: The long weekend the boy spent – subsequent to Agar's Feast – as the guest of the Eton and Slough Constabulary, did little to improve his general attitude, I fear. Nor, I may say, did my reasonable decision to dock him two *per diems* for failing to muster twice at 9 a.m. Indeed, no sooner had I sprung him than he held forth against Eton and what he termed its mumbo-jumbo rituals, his prime complaint being that such had been held in Latin.

As it happened, I was able to confound him thanks to an article I'd read in the *Sunday Telegraph*, in which my friend Sir Worsthorne had defended the retention of the classics on the curriculum at our better public schools, and, as he said, at Eton too.

'The cream of a generation was lost in the mud of Flanders,' Sir Worsthorne wrote. 'Even Etonians went over the top with the *Iliad* in their knapsacks and Athens in their hearts. To protest that such men were statistically not even a trace among the English soldiers killed is to miss the point. At all times the great majority of people have been ignorant of the classics; but the men who mattered, who governed, declared wars, thought and resisted mindless innovation, have always had Latin and Greek.'

All is not lost, surely, when a little Dutch visitor to our shores can create a reverberating English phrase such as 'the *Iliad* in their knapsacks and Athens in their hearts.' Could such an *English* English writer as Dornford Yates have done better, or even Bulldog 'Sapper'?

Floral Dance, The Cornish: As we passed quite inadvertently, through the hilly town of Helston on the way to Land's End, Mrs Root took it upon herself to read from *Beyond the Dart* by my Lord Hailsham, penned, no doubt, between verses composed in the Horatian mode, on this occasion *in re* the Cornish Floral Dance.

'Pom pom, pom-pom-pom,' she suddenly said. 'Pom pom, pom-pom-pom.'

'Do what, Mrs Root?' I said.

'Pom pom, pom-pom-pom,' she said again. 'It's the sound of the band summoning Lord Hailsham to the Cornish Floral Dance.'

My spirits sagged. 'Will this take long?' I said.

'You'll be grateful to me, Henry,' she said. 'It's ever so charming. Listen. "I dressed quickly," writes his Lordship, "and hurried out into a sunny May morning. When the band struck up, the dancers stepped out two by two, hand in hand; then they turned and exchanged partners with the couple behind, executed a quick twirl, and, linking hands with their original partners, continued down the street." '

'Charming indeed,' I said. 'That's it, I take it?'

'Not quite,' said Mrs Root. ' "I caught the eye of a pretty maid," writes Lord Hailsham, "held out my hand, and she came, a little shyly, took hands and, after a while, we became quite good at it. We descended steps still dancing, found ourselves unable to dance in narrow passages, so we just held hands and laughed." '

'I feel a little faint,' I said. 'Could we leave his Lordship dancing up an alley?'

'Almost,' said Mrs Root. 'Listen. It becomes even more charming. "It was all so sweet and innocent and un-modern," says Lord Hailsham. "My partner, who could blush, told me that I was a good dancer. I told her how pretty she was and how much I liked her green

The Cornish Floral Dance: Pom pom, pom-pom-pom! These merry practitioners of the Cornish Floral Dance, having hopped all the way from Land's End, have fetched up outside Truro Cathedral, and now there's nothing for it but to hop all the way back again. They'll know their business best.

hat. She told me that she worked in a draper's shop. The dance ended in front of the Corn Exchange, where my fair one flashed me a glance and said goodbye." '

'Thank God for that,' I said.

Even now, Mrs Root would not be staunched. 'Lord Hailsham says it is a peculiarity of the Cornish Floral Dance that dancers, by tradition, must enter houses and shops by the front door and come out if possible at the back. A householder or shopkeeper regards it as a sign of good fortune when the Floral Dancers enter their premises, and in return they offer drinks and local sweetmeats. It does sound fun, Henry. Couldn't we stop and investigate?'

I'd not in the general run of things wish to skip publicly two by two with Mrs Root, but my people in Birmingham would, after all, expect stills depicting Merrie England, and this daft carry-on sounded such in spades. Plus and further, it so happened that I had a slight thirst, which could be adequately quenched gratis as per the custom of the Floral Dance.

Accordingly, we stopped in Helston and parked the car, made for the high street where I took Mrs Root unusually by the hand. Two skips to the left, two skips to the right, and through the front door as per tradition of a maisonette, in which I availed myself of two bottles of sherry wine and a case of cigars from the lounge-room cabinet – later finding myself in the hands of the constabulary, called to the scene by the owner of the maisonette.

The Cornish Floral Dance, it seems, has not been extant for the last ten years – having been discontinued when, under the spirit of the Enterprise Culture, no doubt, too many shops and homes had been looted by the dancers. I'm unsure whether this is a sign of our national decline or the opposite.

Fool, A: A fool sees not the same tree as a wise man sees.

Foreign Exile: I had to bring the boy up short one day – we were in Folkstone, to be precise – as he extolled the virtues of life in foreign parts.

'Wouldn't it be nice, Mr Root,' he said, 'if we could hop on the ferry, finding ourselves an hour and a half later on the Continent.'

'It bloody well wouldn't,' I said. 'Given a choice, no true English-man would opt for freedom abroad against prison on his native soil. As my friend Sir Worsthorne has accurately observed, "The ancients were wiser than us in recognising exile as the harshest punishment of all. Two centuries ago, a thief, when taken, would have preferred incarceration to foreign exile." '

'I'm sure you're right, Mr Root,' said the boy. 'And no doubt Mr Ronald Biggs, the celebrated train robber, agrees with Mr Worsthorne, even as he lives out his Brazilian nightmare, stuck on some sunny beach with the dusky maiden of his choice.'

Irony, was it? Just in case, I clipped him round the ear.

'My sympathies,' I said, 'are with the train driver. An unfashionable point of view these days.' (*See also* GIBBET, THE.)

Football, A Political: No true Englishman cares to be a political football. (*See also* FRACAS, A; *and* SLOPES, SLIPPERY.)

Fracas, A: Returning home one day from an outing to the Mendips, (they'd still not gone away), I was caught up in a fracas with Alderman Entwistle (rtd). The fellow was on my land, if you please, checking, he said, on whether my games room was being dismantled as per council edict 6578b.

I turned to the boy. 'Call an ambulance,' I said.

Entwistle seemed quite startled. 'Are you poorly, Mr Root?' he said.

'No,' I said. 'But you'll be needing one within thirty seconds unless you reverse pronto off my land.'

The fool stood firm. 'I hope,' he said, 'that you're not going to add the crime of common assault to what at the moment is only the civil tort of slander.'

He'd asked for it, the little Hitler. Up on the toes, a feint with the left, a right below the ribs and Alderman Entwistle went down like a sack of meal. You never lose it.

I helped him off the premises, but now indeed I'm up for assault as well as slander. I'm not too bothered, and Doreen, the girl, is standing firm.

'You're a political football, Daddy,' she said, 'a pawn in a power struggle being conducted by the council. You're a victim of injustice, and, as such, you must be defended by Shakespeare and Shakespeare.'

'And who might they be?' I said. 'It's a name with a certain resonance to it, I'll grant them that.'

'Friends of mine from university,' Doreen said. 'Community lawyers, trading in Hackney. They recently defended the Highbury Two. They'll fight the system for you. They're the best in the business at defending the small man.'

I was unaccustomed as yet to being referred to as 'a small man', but I bowed for once to the girl's greater experience in the matter of political footballs. I have an appointment to meet Shakespeare and Shakespeare next week. (*See also* SHAKESPEARE AND SHAKESPEARE.)

Frontiers, *Our*: A most interesting meeting with the little woman in charge at VAT and Excise – not that we saw her. She was out – bagging trans-Continental drug-fiends, we can only hope or, with Gloria Hunniford, planning a media blitz against cannabis abusers – but an underling assured me that, as per promises given by Lady Finchley before her sad betrayal, our frontiers would be maintained at all times, with a full SAS presence and stop-and-search of ethnic minorities.

After the meeting, I got into an argument with the boy, of course.

'It's outrageous,' he said, 'that eighty-seven per cent of the people stopped and searched at our frontiers are black – be they doctors, lawyers or university professors. It's barefaced racism.'

'Nonsense,' I said. 'Racism implies prejudice, and prejudice doesn't come into it. It's a simple fact that ninety per cent of the people found to be carrying drugs are black.'

'Of *course* they're black!' said the boy. 'Only black people get searched!'

'And quite right too,' I said, 'since, by your own statistics, it is they who are carrying drugs.'

I'd exposed his logic-chopping yet again.

Garfield, Det-Sgt Ronnie: Surely it's a sign of our sad national decline that Prince Edward's personal detective should have been required, at Gordonstoun, to be bullied for the Prince (toasted and so forth in front of fires – *see* BULLYING), then, at Jesus College, Cambridge, to play rugger for him, date Spanish 'models' and sit his exams – getting a respectable 2.2. The debate continues.

That said, Det-Sgt Garfield drew the line at taking the Royal Marine Commando course on Edward's behalf, preferring, instead, to join the Very Exciting Theatre Company, disguised as the Prince, running errands and making the tea for Sir Lloyd Webber, the balloon-faced cellist.

It is not generally known that Edward is now an undercover member of the SAS, whereas ex-Det-Sgt Garfield, thanks to the duffing-up he got at Gordonstoun, will shortly have his first play performed by Sir Branagh's strolling players.

Giants, Gentle: Gentle Giants are, by definition, English. You'd not meet a Welsh Gentle Giant, though Graham Price, a prop forward from Pontypool built like a Polish sausage, is a borderline case, I'd grant you, as is Gordon Brown, the potato-faced Scot from the Edinburgh Academicals.

That said, sheer size is a necessary, though not sufficient, defining characteristic. Bill Beaumont, for example, is a Gentle Giant. The big lad, Botham, on the other hand, isn't a Gentle Giant. Gentle Giants are not caught three-in-a-bed in the Caribbean.

'What about Frank Bruno?' said the boy.

I was thunderstruck. 'He wasn't, was he?' I said. 'I'd not heard that.'

'I meant, is he a Gentle Giant?'

'Certainly not,' I said. 'As I explained, Gentle Giants are by definition, English. Frank Bruno may be one of Nature's Gentlemen, which is an entirely different matter.'

'He's a coconut,' said the boy.

'You'd not say that to his face,' I said. 'Or if you did, you'd fetch up in casualty with your various common parts in traction.'

'Violence,' said the boy, 'is the last resort of the inarticulate.'

I gave him inarticulate. I clipped him round the ear.

'If you don't stop clipping him round the ear,' said Mrs Root, 'you'll find yourself at the wrong end of a caring hot-line.'

'I heard you the first time, thank you, Mrs Root,' I said. (*See also* NATURE'S GENTLEMEN; *and* SCRUM, COLLAPSING THE.)

Gibbet, The: Driving one day to Winchester on an English summer afternoon (there to research Gunners Hole and so forth), we stumble inadvertently upon a gibbet on a hill.

We stop to investigate, discover that this is the notorious Coombe Gallows, kept in repair by the good people of Coombe as a tourist attraction.

'Cottage teas,' says an illustrated legend appended to the gibbet, 'can be obtained in Coombe. Kiddies' menu provided.'

Some may find the retention of a gibbet to advertise kiddies' teas a trifle ghoulish, but I recall an anecdote told in the Garrick Club one day by Warden Sparrow of All Souls, as was.

'Some shipwrecked sailors,' said Warden Sparrow, 'were approaching an island in an open boat. Scanning the coastline, they suddenly perceived something standing against the sky. Was it a tree? No. As they drew nearer, they could make out what it was. A gibbet, with a dead body hanging from it. "Thank God!" cried the sailors. "A civilised country!" '

That said, the cottage tea served in Coombe, turned out to be no better than that dished up by the mad old biddies on Parker's Nose. Happily, as we know, such establishments are shortly to be closed down, by EC statute 76854B. (*See also* JOKES, DONNISH.)

Glyndebourne: To Glyndebourne on the opera special from Victoria, myself in white tie and topper, and equipped with Hasselblad and strobe, the boy in a lounge suit, if you please, Mrs Root attired by Bourne and Hollingsworth (Esher Branch).

Since Sir Wheatcroft, the little opera buff, was in our carriage, I

The Gibbet: A little Dutch tourist receives a salutary reminder of a time when wrongdoers got their just desserts. In Merrie England, a footpad would have found himself suspended from a gibbet; now we'd be told that his victims were guiltier than he was; and that he should be rehoused in a salubrious suburb at our expense and his needs attended to by a team of 'caring' social workers.

pretended not to know them – least of all when Mrs Root offered me a slice of pork pie and Nescafé from a Thermos.

'Not at the moment, madam,' I said. 'Been in this country long, have you?'

I turned to Sir Wheatcroft, suggested with a lift of the eyebrow that the *opéra bouffe* attracts all sorts these days, inferred that there was a picnic in the offing on the lawn.

'Music's all the more affecting, wouldn't you say,' I said, 'for being heard in an agreeable setting? "Wolfgang's muse brought to earth thrice weekly" – I'm quoting Levin here, the one with legs – "twixt Bollinger and salmon pâté, by the Divine Songbird herself!" '

Oh yes, I know the parlance on the opera train, and, later, in the auditorium. Once seated, I followed the action through my naval binoculars, laughed loudly at foreign operatic jokes, beat time, sang along, set up my Hasselblad and strobe ('Don't mind me – researching for Central Television'), at the interval wandered into the private parts for an encouraging word with Dame Kanawa, the little Maori.

'Settling in all right, are you, Dame Kanawa?' I said. 'Don't mind Sir Solti, by the way, who recently dismissed you, I believe, by inferring sneeringly that you'd be a good person to go shopping with. What's wrong with that? In Dr Johnson's view a man is better pleased when there are a range of groceries in the fridge than when his wife has an aria up her sleeve. Don't worry about Sir Solti. He's foreign. You're ethnic, which is an entirely different matter.'

Having put the little Maori at her ease, I returned to Esher – only twigging on arrival that I'd quit at half-time, leaving the boy and Mrs Root in Sussex. I'd not missed much, I don't suppose.

Grasses: Here's a conundrum: does a true Englishman finger his neighbour? In my day, and in my neck of the woods, you didn't finger your neighbour. Had you fingered your neighbour, you'd have gone head first into the nearest bollard or upside down into a municipal rubbish tip.

That said, my friend Richard Ingrams has, for the past thirty years or more, made a good living fingering miscreants – and he's a true Englishman, if anyone is. There attaches to him, does there not, a reassuring aroma of wet labradors and country matters on his trousers; he wears in all weathers two pairs of knitted socks and attends lunchtime organ concerts in his tweeds. He'll be the first common informer to get a knighthood, mark my words.

Plus and further, there's the matter of Esther Rantzen, the little watchdog, urging children to grass up their parents on a hot-line and neighbours to finger one another down the line. In my day, you didn't finger your neighbour. You led with the knuckle and stood up close, you breathed on the back of his neck – and I said as much one day to the boy and Mrs Root.

'But you fingered Alderman Entwistle, Mr Root,' said the boy. 'You put up posters all over Esher saying that he hadn't paid his Poll Tax.'

I was astonished, frankly. 'That's an entirely different matter,' I said. 'We're researching a five-part docudrama here and, as I've observed before, the makers of docudramas have rights over and above Joe Public. A maker of a docudrama can finger and infer as the mood, and his artistic leanings, take him.'

'Trial by television, Mr Root,' the boy said. 'We're on a slippery slope here.'

'I'll be the judge of slippery slopes,' I said. 'Plus in any case, you've not confronted my main thrust: is the Rantzen woman's hot line valid? Come to that, can she be counted as truly English?'

'In fact,' said the boy, 'she isn't English in any way. Rantzen means "old boot" in German.'

I didn't know that. The boy had caught me unawares. Now I don't know what to think. Next I'll discover that 'Sir Ingrams' means cattle turd in Dutch. (*See also* JOE PUBLIC; *and* SLOPES, SLIPPERY.)

Hands, A Safe Pair of: We English admire a safe pair of hands, be it in the slips or on the front bench. Oddly enough, a safe pair of hands is signified, in the slips, by raising the voice through an octave or two (as per Gatting and the portly soprano, Gooch) and, on the front bench, by lowering it, as per Lady Finchley and the Foreign Secretary, Sir Hurd.

Sir Hurd's all right. I'm uncertain still about the sledge-green topcoat, but the peculiar voice is sound, suggesting bottom in a crisis.

Senior Tories, it must be said, lack a safe pair of hands, not least Lamont, the little failed Chancellor with a quiff.

A *masseuse* in the basement, was it? I'm aware that he was ignorant of the woman's presence, but that won't do. Just because you haven't seen a *masseuse* in your basement it doesn't mean that there isn't one such trading there – quite possibly wearing a basque in the early afternoon and entrapping such of your colleagues as lack a safe pair of hands.

I check my basement against *masseuses* once a month. (*See also* BASQUES; *and* MELLOR, DAVID.)

Harvey-Jones, Sir John: The day arrives when Sir Jones is to deliver his report in the matter of Henry Root Wet Fish. I drive to the office in a state of some excitement, envisaging Mortimer's face when he twigs that it's an early bath for him.

Arrived on site, I'm momentarily discommoded to discover Mortimer's Volvo in my parking space. I ask an attendant I'd not seen before what this might signify, and he tells me it's a new practice initiated by Sir Jones.

'Excellent!' I cry. 'First come, first served and the devil take the hindmost! We live in the unsentimental nineties, after all. The man's red hot. Name?'

'Perkins, Sir.'

'Right, Perkins! Move this Volvo! Jump to it!'

I'm next confounded by a new security system, likewise initiated, I imagine, by Sir Jones. None of my plastic entry cards suffices, obliging me to summon a receptionist whom, like Perkins, I'd not seen before. She denies me ingress, asks me who I am.

'Excellent!' I cry. 'One can't be too careful. There'll be freezing methods here we'll not want in the hands of Johnnie Frog. I'm Henry Root. I own the firm.'

'How do I know that?' she says. 'Wait here.'

She closes the door in my face, compelling me to kick my heels in the outer vestibule while she checks my identity against her newly encoded records. I'm impressed, I must say. Sir Jones isn't as silly as he looks.

There's better to come. Once I'm granted ingress, it transpires that, under Sir Jones's way of doing things, I'm not one of those cleared to ramble solo round the building and am therefore escorted to the boardroom by the new receptionist. On the way, I ask her what happened to old Mrs Jenkins, my secretary for thirty years.

'Sir John had to let her go,' this new girl said. 'Her face didn't fit in with the firm's new image.'

'Quite right,' I say. 'I never cared for her myself.'

He's dynamite, Sir Jones. We reach the boardroom, where Sir Jones, in the chair, is about to deliver his report. The assembled directors look nervous, as well they might. I wink at Sir Jones; behind Mortimer's back, draw a finger across my throat, signifying that he's first for the axeman's blade.

Sir Jones smiles in my direction. I smile back, am still smiling when, after a preamble about dead wood, outmoded habits which resist necessary innovation, Sir Jones identifies me as the drag on the business.

I'm presented with a commemorative memento – a model of my grandfather, Henry 'Cannonball' Root's, first whelk stall – and am then escorted off the premises. I'm surprised, I must say. I drive back to Esher in a state of shock – have recovered, however, by the time I get there.

'How was your day, Henry?' says Mrs Root.

'Excellent,' I say. 'I was fired.'

'Oh I say,' she says.

'Never mind "oh I say",' I say. 'Sir Jones has given me a sharp idea. I see now how he got his knighthood. He pitches up at an old-time enterprise and fires the chairman. I could do that. I know dead wood. I'm dead wood myself, remember, recently identified as such by Sir Jones. I shall become a troubleshooter myself, in association with Sir Jones, perhaps.'

'Is that wise, Henry?' says Mrs Root. 'After all, he's fired you once already.'

'Lightning doesn't strike twice in the same place, Mrs Root,' I say. 'I know what I'm doing.'

And so I do. Outside my house I have already erected a large sign which reads: 'Henry Root and Sir Jones – Troubleshooters'. A knighthood's in the bag, I think. (*See also* HONOURS.)

Henry VIII: The changing shape of Englishmen. In Tudor times, men on average attained a height of only 5ft 3. Sir Thomas More (*background*), the little Chancellor, was merely 5ft 2, which means that bluff Prince Hal – albeit inflated by *bombinade* and appetite, and therefore as wide as he was tall – was only 4ft 8. Small wonder that he was bested by the Mayor of Flanders on a foreign field.

Henry V: The victor at Agincourt, here appropriately portrayed by that most English of actors (the comic diction, thin legs and peculiar carriage), Sir Kenneth Branagh. Coincidentally, Sir Branagh is, aptly, only 5ft 4, which meant that all scenes between him and Lady Branagh (5ft 8) — here playing the little French Princess — had to be enacted sitting down, or with Sir Branagh standing on a tea-chest.

Heritage, English: The recent supplantation at English Heritage of Lord Montagu, the little antique car collector, by my old friend Lord Stevens of the *Daily Express* and so forth can only augur well, I think, for our castles and other crumbling sites.

I like an old house as much as the next man (*see* HOMES, STATELY), not least if a small contribution to the upkeep of its roof might assist in the matter of my peerage. Thus, I called on my old friend Lord Stevens at the *Express* one day, rattling change in either pocket.

'He won't keep you long,' his secretary said.

'Good,' I said. 'We go back a long way, Lord Stevens and I. Since he was given *Queen*, in fact, by old Lord Hulton as a birthday present. Most dub him an ill-mannered braggart, liable at the drop of a hat to turn plum red and start throwing people out of windows, but I admire the man.'

The girl seemed interested, so I pressed on with my dissertation.

'He was brought in here, you know, by Lord Cunard of Hammersmith, the little builder, to sort the unions out. He did that quickly enough. Brought production to a halt. And a good thing too in my opinion. I'm a *Telegraph* man myself, though Mrs Root swears by the *Daily Mail*. How do you draw with Lady Bollard, then?'

The girl seemed startled, temporarily suspended the filing of her nails.

'Lady who?' she said.

'Bollard,' I said. 'The editor of the *Sunday Express*. Some say she isn't as pleasant as she looks.'

'Oh – you mean Eve Pollard,' said the girl. 'I never see her.'

'I'm not surprised,' I said. 'Away on freebies, for the most part, or appearing in TV game-shows. He's not thrown you out of the window yet? I'm talking about my friend, Lord Stevens now.'

'Not yet,' said the girl, who, I could see, was enjoying our chat. 'Ah – here he is now.'

'Stevens, my dear old friend!' I cried. 'Here's a fiver for English Heritage . . . goats and monkeys! You've lost weight!'

And so he had. Once he had resembled a side of beef in a striped shirt; now he was little bigger than a weasel.

'Who are you?' asked this shadow of my former friend.

'Sir Root,' I said. 'Here on behalf of Central Television to donate five pounds to English Heritage.'

'I'm afraid you've got the wrong man,' he said. 'You want Jocelyn Stevens.'

'In that case,' I said, 'I'll have my fiver back.'

An embarrassing tussle ensued, with me tugging at one end of the fiver and this *soi-disant* Lord Stevens not only tugging at the other end but begging me to let him keep it. Those with shares in *Express* Newspapers would do well to unload them, if they can. That's my reading of the situation.

Holiday, The English Summer: Does it survive? In my day – before the package holiday for all – it wasn't two weeks in the so-called Balearics, catching dysentery and watching fat Germans jog and overeat. It was a week on the south coast with Mum and Dad and Auntie Mabel.

To test the matter out, I ruled that we'd visit Broadstairs on an August afternoon.

'This will be agreeable,' I said. 'Mr Pastry entertaining the kiddies on the pier. Lads fishing with their fathers. Old gents in deck-chairs with their mouths hanging open and hankies on their heads. Fat ladies tucking their skirts into their stays and paddling in the English Channel.'

The English Summer Holiday: Time was when the English could recline and paddle on a family beach, unembarrassed by nude vicars, lager louts and topless away-day exhibitionists (*left*). Now (*right*), the beckoning shingle has disappeared completely under fairground wheels and dodgem cars.

Oh yes, it all came back. Sand castle competitions. Donkey rides. Beach cricket. Crazee golf. Candy floss. Uncle Jim spending a fortune in a 'What the Butler Saw' machine. Nothing wrong with that. Healthy English vulgarity, nothing more.

'As evening falls,' I said, 'a uniformed brass ensemble plays Ivor Novello extracts on a podium. "We'll Gather Lilacs", was it? I'll eat my hat if so-called Jacques Delors has been able to subsume such a typically English scene.'

I'd have done better not to mention my hat. It wasn't at all like that. *En route*, it's five-mile tailbacks now. The way blocked by mangled coaches, held hostage by crop-haired youths in building-site boots. Knife fights at traffic lights. Screaming babies swollen with wasp bites. Caravan sites with great reeking women queuing for the only turbo-toilet. Common girls from Harlow New Town offer themselves arse up over breakwaters to apprentice mechanics on probation.

As evening falls, twelve-year-old girls on day release from a remand home tout pin-up pictures of Axl Rose with pornographic captions, attempt to fit up the apprentice mechanics on an indecency charge. The common girls from Harlow New Town dance round their handbags in a disco in a mood of absent-minded appetite, later receive a hammering behind the bandstand by local roustabouts.

We return to Esher in a sombre mood.

'Pass the pork pie, Mrs Root,' I said.

The boy handed me my hat, I don't know why.

Homes, Stately: As we approached the Palace of Blenheim on an English summer afternoon, Mrs Root took it upon herself to give us some info *in re* the building of the place.

'After Marlborough humbled the French,' she said, 'at Blenheim in Bavaria, a grateful nation wished to honour their Captain-General with a great memorial. It was decided by Queen Anne that she and Parliament would build at their joint cost a grand house in Oxfordshire to be called the Palace of Blenheim. Designed by the playwright, Sir John Vanbrugh, it took seventeen years to be completed, with the result that Marlborough himself never saw it. What an agreeable, and peculiarly English, irony!'

'Never mind irony, Mrs Root,' I said. 'In all likelihood, Sir Vanbrugh, the little playwright, was beset by an officious alderman next door who blocked his permissions at every turn.'

(As I've observed before, I think, I'll not use my platform here to pursue a purely private vendetta against my own next-door neighbour,

Stately Homes: Blenheim Palace, my friend the Duke of Marlborough's country place. I see that the Marquess of Blandford, his troubled heir, has already anticipated his inheritance by planting incognito marijuana plants among His Lordship's more classically topiarian effects. I'll not be the one to tip his father off. That's not my way.

Alderman Entwistle (rtd), or to call the man a horse or little Hitler – except when it's relevant. To do such would not be my way.)

'In fact,' said Mrs Root, 'in the absence of Marlborough on the Continent, work was supervised by his wife, Sarah, who didn't get along with Vanbrugh. Hence the delay.'

It's a wonder the building was ever completed. The unfortunate Captain-General was clamped, it seems to me, in what we'd now call a double whammy. A woman and a theatrical in charge of the erection, and an officious alderman next door.

'Mind the loins, Mrs Root,' I said.

Mrs Root seemed quite startled. 'The loins, Henry? What loins?'

'The loins of Longleat, Mrs Root,' I said.

'Don't you mean lions?' she said.

'No, I mean loins,' I said. 'An amusing reference, I gather, to the late Lord Bath's boy, Weymouth – as was – so dubbed on account of his habit of keeping women in the grounds. Wifelets, he calls them.'

'This isn't Longleat,' said the boy. 'This is Blenheim.'

'And a good thing too,' I said. 'We'd not want to be confronted by a loin, still less by a bearded hippy in a dress. If we meet the Duke, don't mention the boy.'

As we negotiated the long drive, I expatiated for the others' benefit on the habits of the English upper classes, pointing out that they characteristically dress down – the upshot being that chance visitors such as ourselves as a rule mistake his Lordship for the gardener.

'We'll not make that mistake,' I said. 'That gnarled derelict over there – tending the roses in his ancestral trousers – he'll be the Duke of Bath.'

'Marlborough,' said the boy.

'Or him,' I said. 'Either way, his trousers will have been in the family for three hundred years or more.' I approached the old boy and tapped him on the shoulder. 'Henry Root,' I said. 'Pardon my breath, it was eggs for tea. Sorry to hear about the boy. I gather he wears a dress and keeps women in the grounds.'

The boy Partridge tugged at my sleeve, muttered *sotto voce* in my ear. 'That's the Marquess of Bath,' he said. 'I keep *telling* you. This is the Duke of Marlborough, Blandford's father.'

It was my turn to apprise the boy *sotto voce*. 'Don't mention Blandford,' I said. 'How many times do I have to tell you?'

The Duke looked us up and down, shortly enquired whether we were circus folk. *Circus* folk? I wasn't having that.

'In fact,' I said, 'we're researching Merrie England for Central Television. A prime-time six-parter fronted by myself. Play your cards right, your Grace, and you could land a cameo role. We'll not want the boy, thank you very much.'

'Show business, eh?' said the Duke. 'You'll have to use the artistes' entrance. Round the back. And I'm the gardener.'

'I can see that,' I said. 'And never mind round the back. I'm not using the same entrance as Sir Mark and his lady. We'll be off now, thank you very much. Kindly convey my condolences to his Grace *in re* the boy.'

We departed at this point, satisfied that the place still stood. (*See also* BLANDFORD, THE MARQUESS OF; *and* SONS, PROBLEMATIC ELDER.)

Honours: I have an argument over breakfast with the girl, Doreen, *in re* honours. She dubs my desire for one as snobbish and hypocritical, further suggesting that this country will be the sick man of Europe while outdated patronage survives.

'I see,' I say. 'And what, pray, about the French?'

I'd not normally cite the French as an example, but the girl walks headfirst into my trap.

'What about them?' she says.

'Had you been in Paris in '68,' I say, 'you'd have revolted with the students, I imagine, taunting the *gendarmerie* and igniting thunder-flashes underneath their horses.'

'I certainly would,' she says. 'The struggle against oppression knows no frontiers.'

'I see,' I say. 'And yet the French are more class-conscious than the English will ever be. You'll not be aware, I take it, that in spite of *Madame La Guillotine* the Second Estate survives, indeed flourishes in France. I read recently in the *Telegraph* that there were twelve thousand noble families in France in 1789; today there are twenty-two thousand!

'Since no new peerages have been created since 1830, this might seem impossible, but the explanation is simple. The new aristocracy, with typical Gallic cheek, has created itself! By paying as little as five thousand pounds a year, families can buy a title from an organisation called the *Association de la Noblesse Française*, which thereafter will hire you a black tie and pumps for formal occasions and advise you on points of etiquette – such as correct placement at a *thé dansant* and the avoidance of *faux pas* such as shovelling *petits pois* straight into your mouth off a knife.

'Had my friend Lord Archer, the little airport novelist, been French he could have been a Count twenty years ago *and* have made unscheduled drops at Victoria Station. What have you got to say to that?'

This time, I'd confounded the girl and no mistake, but she hadn't had enough. 'I am fully aware of the hypocrisy and class-consciousness of the French,' she said, 'which is *precisely* why I'd have taken to the streets in '68. Thank you for arguing my case so cogently.'

Damn me, I'd been confounded by the girl. That said, my reference earlier to my friend Lord Archer had given me a sharp idea concerning my own intentions in the matter of a peerage. Unless I was much mistaken, the little sprinter had, during his years in the wilderness, kept himself on the social map by giving weekly parties. I remembered too that Sir David Frost only kicked up after he had thrown a celebrity get-together in Claridges' breakfast-lounge.

'We'll give a party, Mrs Root,' I said. 'With the PM's new classless honours system – gongs by public nomination – it is more important than ever to scratch the appropriate backs. It worked for Sir Frost and for my friend Lord Archer. Champagne and *vol-au-vents* served to his betters in his penthouse flat and he gets a peerage notwithstanding.'

'Notwithstanding what, Henry?' says Mrs Root.

'We'll not go into that,' I say. 'It will be a marquee on the lawn and a strict tempo dance ensemble. Sir Root at home. Myself waltzing with Sir Jones's lady. I'll plan the guest list now.'

And so I did, drawing up a list of likely referees *in re* my peerage and dropping them a small *doucement* with their invite. 'You nominate me, and I'll nominate you. Nod's as good as a wink. See you on the 26th.' (*See also* PARTY, THE; *and* WEATHER, LUCKY WITH THE.)

Hunt, The: Keen as ever to participate in the rich contrasts of country ways, we ride with the Beaufort – more accurately, take up station at a researcher's distance, and in a country conveyance hired for the day.

What a magnificent scene! Local girls pass round stirrup cups and a man with a bucket of fox's offal incites the hounds. A jackass in hunting pink ('Bunter' Somerset, is it?) blows a horn and off we go. Farmers, fat women, pubescent girls, Saturday *nouveaux* down for the day, sadistic majors with Swaine and Adeney discipline whips, two duffle-coated infiltrators from the Anti Bloodsports League and, taking up the rear, ourselves in the hired conveyance.

At the first fence, the fat women go over their horses' heads. The other riders rein in behind a magnificent huntswoman who rises provocatively to the trot. To hold position behind her straining jodhpurs, they plough through hedges into private gardens, churn up the lawn and send croquet players flying.

I flatten a henhouse with the hired conveyance, proceed with chickens adhering to the wheels. Country folk would understand.

The infiltrators lay a false trail which leads towards the steep edge of a gravel pit. The hunt plunges twenty feet into dirty water, their horses' legs beating for purchase in the empty air. The infiltrators snigger in their duffle-coats.

The field straggles out across eight hundred acres in the failing light. The jackass with the horn plays 'Colonel Bogey'. A dismounted girl steps into a hole and is savaged by a badger. The boy faints. I shoot the badger, which dies at my feet of a broken heart. The boy faints again.

The Hunt: Tally Ho! Members of the Beaufort sportingly give hunt saboteurs a half-hour start. The horses champ at the bit, the hounds — enraged by the smell of a duffel-coat — are ready for the off. The average bag, I'm told, is one fox and six saboteurs.

'Country ways,' I explain. 'Badgers have to be disciplined. Each day in the Highlands, the Queen Mother bites into a badger turd to see which way the wind's blowing, then, for discipline reasons, she shoots the badger. Country folk would understand.'

At last, the hounds corner the fox, which explodes in a ball of fur and faeces. This will make excellent prime-time slottage for those with country stomachs. The moustachioed MFH then sticks the fox's penis into the ear of the first pubescent girl to arrive at the kill. The boy faints for the third time. Weeping men cover their faces and shoot their broken horses. Hounds are rewarded with pet cats and tropical birds. The infiltrators are suddenly uncovered and whipped off the premises with cries of 'Tally Ho!'

'Don't concern yourself,' I say to the boy. 'They enjoy being hunted as much as the fox does.'

A limping infiltrator is caught by the hunt. 'My God!' cries the boy. 'What will happen to her, Mr Root?'

'Much the same as happened to the fox,' I say. 'We're privileged to see it.'

I aim the Hasselblad and strobe, but, to my embarrassment, the boy intervenes on the girl's behalf, attempts to rescue the little anarchist from the country intentions of the hunt.

The baying huntsmen round on us, lash at us with their Swaine and Adeney discipline whips. I make it to the hired conveyance seconds ahead of an infuriated major. I return to Esher, thoroughly exhilarated. Only to discover when I get there that I've left the boy behind. An excellent day's research.

Ice: The Swiss may yodel in the pine trees, shine on the Cresta
Run and so forth, but we English prevail on ice. The little
policeman in a tutu and the other one — Jane Torville, is it? —
ice-skate for England to Ravel's *Bolero.*

Iconoclasm, Acceptable: We English frown on iconoclasm unless it's constructive. We have iconoclasts, of course. Malcolm Muggeridge, he was one, but look what happened to him. Mike Yarwood, he was another. His targets were the first to laugh, as is the case with all the best satire.

Dave Allen, the little comedian, he's another. Irreverent without being funny. Tasteful without giving offence. That's all right.

'Only joking, madam! May God go with you.'

Prime-time iconoclasm. Nothing wrong with that. The lampoonist must respect his victim – something which our younger comedians seem to have forgotten.

Industry, British: What an indictment of successive governments that young folk, keen to thrive in British industry, would do best – unless possessing a tutu and artistic merit on ice (see ICE) – to set up shop trading in compassion, abortion, race relations or euthanasia.

That said, British Industry is not without muscle while such as myself and Sir Jones survive. My own career as a troubleshooter is off to a flying start. Brochures, outlining my services in colour, have been distributed, and a range of small, local enterprises has already benefitted from my advice.

My *modus* has been to arrive suddenly among them, thereafter identifying dead wood, those too ostentatiously inflating their expenses and such as should have been confined already in a home.

'Don't mind me,' I say. 'Sir Root, of "Root and Sir Jones". I'm here to turn your business round. You're fired, madam.'

Thus, Mr Patel, my local newsagent, has been disencumbered of his extended family – grandparents, uncles, aunts and so forth are back on the banana boat from whence they came – and of the two mad biddies who, for fifty years, have run a sweetshop on the corner, one has been committed as incontinent, the other has half her shares, I have the rest.

Plus and further, of course, I have negotiated a profitable *quid pro quo* with the home my dear old mother's in. I get a 'drink' for each remaindered biddy tipped their way.

Intellect, The: I have – only temporarily, I trust – lost the services of the boy: the upshot of his ricking his back while washing the Jaguar in the drive.

'Put your feet up for half an hour and it will be as good as new,' I said.

'What if it isn't?' he said.

'In that case,' I said, 'Mrs Root can wash the Jaguar.'

By the evening, he was doubled up with pain and, since he was of little use like this, I was obliged to deposit him at a local hospital – where, for some reason, I happened to observe while waiting that we English, alone among Europeans, understand that the intellect is a poor instrument for discovering what goes on in the human heart. Plain obvious, you'd have thought, but the boy, in spite of the pain he was in, had something to say, of course.

'The heart, Mr Root,' he said, 'is a muscle – ouch! – like any other in the human body and, since what goes on in there is simply the operation of a pump, the intellect, backed up by surgical technology, would seem to be precisely the most appropriate instrument for discovering it.'

'I see,' I said. 'You're suggesting, are you, that a mere pump could have produced so much poetry and music of enduring and very English beauty? I refer to Sir Newbolt, the patriotic versifier, and Sir Webber, the balloon-faced cellist. Is that your inference?'

'No,' said the boy, 'it isn't. Do you think the doctor will be able to see me soon?'

'Never mind that,' I said. 'What is your inference, then?'

'I'm saying that it's not the heart but the mind which produces human artefacts.'

He'd fallen into my trap, of course. 'I see,' I said. 'But I have it on your own assertion that the "mind", as such, doesn't exist.' He was hoist with his own petard, I thought.

The boy was thunderstruck. 'I'm hoist with my own petard, Mr Root,' he said.

Irony, was it? To be on the safe side, I clipped him round the ear – inadvertently knocking him off his chair and thereby rendering him not only hoist with his own petard but, when the doctor arrived, hoist in traction too.

'Oh dear,' said the boy, 'my BUPA's lapsed.'

'I thought it was just your back,' I said.

'I mean, my policy's run out.'

'In that case,' I said, 'we can't afford the treatment. I'd better take you home.'

Since he was stretched out as rigid as a board, I placed him on the roof of the Jaguar and drove him back to Esher. I saw no reason why I should pay for him to be treated as a private patient.

Intellectuals, Left-Wing: Most left-wing intellectuals have been educated at the expense of the very system they seek to overthrow. What a telling refutation of their principles, moreover, that they so rapidly eschew the trappings of their disadvantaged backgrounds!

'Mark this,' I said to the boy one day. 'Were Mrs Scargill, Bernie Grant and Dame Jackson to stop for a picnic lunch on a miners' march I'll wager you this: the *vol-au-vents* would have come from Fortnums.'

'A theory is not refuted, Mr Root,' he said, 'by the fact that those who profess it to be true fail to live by its consequences. The statements, "I am opposed to the public school system" and "I sent my son to Eton" do not logically contradict each other.'

I gave him logically contradict. Since he was still in traction – more accurately, stretched out on my settee – and since it is no fun flattening a lad who is already on his back, I eschewed the backhander in the face on this occasion, satisfying myself instead with a verbal head butt.

'Since I believe in the prompt discharge of my financial obligations,' I said, 'I propose to dock you a week's worth of emoluments. Nor, I think you'll agree, am I thereby contradicting myself in logic.'

The boy moaned softly and closed his eyes – an acknowledgement, I take it, that I'd out-argued him yet again.

Irony: A two-edged sword, as the boy is discovering to his cost.

Joe Public: We English forget at our peril that Joe Public has the last word.

'Are you Joe Public, Mr Root?' asked the boy, as we drove to the Mendips on an English summer afternoon.

'Certainly not,' I said. 'I'm on the other side of the footlights altogether, a "performer", in the best sense of the word. An opinion former, a mover and shaker – you'll forgive the parlance.'

'But you like to have the last word,' he said.

I gave him last word. I clipped him round the ear.

Jokes, Donnish: Not all the Academy, I'm glad to say, has been swamped in recent years by the isms and perversions issuing from Cambridge. In Oxford, particularly, the English sense of humour has survived, as is evidenced by Warden Sparrow's many jokes, the best of which have been cited by his more perceptive obituarists.

'Listen to this,' I said to the boy, as we drove back from the Mendips (they'd not gone away). 'I'm quoting from Warden Sparrow's obituary in *The Times*, by my friend Lord Stevas of Fawsley, the little constitutionalist.

' "I would remind you of Mr Sparrow's wireless address of 1968, *Revolting Students*," writes Lord Fawsley, since it contains one – or two – of his imperishable jokes. Some Essex students (who else!) had been violently drunk on whisky. ' "Grant's whisky, one may presume!" was Mr Sparrow's incomparable comment." '

'Pray cease, Mr Root,' the boy said. 'Another such joke and I may crack a rib or rick my back again.'

What was this? Taking the rise, was he? I gave him a long look, but he had assumed a poker player's mien. I decided to continue.

'I'll take that risk,' I said. ' "Grant's, the distillers, were upset,"

Donnish Jokes: Having advised Her Majesty on loopholes in the tax laws, Lord Fawsley of Stevas, the little *boulevardier*, leaves the Palace to pace the streets, or, as he prefers to say, take his evening constitutional.

writes Lord Fawsley, "so the great man added a footnote to his address, suggesting instead Teacher's whisky! A double to which we should all raise our glasses. That said, and even while tears of laughter are pouring down our cheeks, we would be wiser than we are were we not to forget this: these are jokes, certainly, but they are not the less serious for that, and they are the jokes of a trained mind." What do you say to that, young Partridge?'

'Anything left of the pork pie, Mrs Root?' he said.

He'd not said that before. Now I don't know what to think. (*See also* ACADEMICS.)

Jury-Rigging: An abuse of British justice. (*See also* JUSTICE, BRITISH.) As Lord Hailsham had it: 'A fox should not be of a jury at a goose's trial.' Thus, one of Lord Denning's imperishable judgements, for which I make no apology for citing here.

'It was a coloured area in Bristol,' summed up Lord Denning. 'A few of the good Bristol police force went to investigate some of the wrongful acts being committed there. They were set upon by the coloured folk. Twelve of the wrongdoers were arrested. They were charged with a riot. A riot it certainly was. They were to be tried by jury. By using their right to challenge they were able to get five coloured folk on the jury. The jury thus constituted acquitted eight of the accused. That, in my opinion, was an abuse of the right to challenge.'

Dissertating for the benefit of the boy one day on the subject of British justice, I drew this judgement to his attention.

'But Mr Root,' he said, 'you have refuted yourself out of your own mouth.'

I didn't like the sound of that. 'How so?' I said.

'If it's the case,' he said, 'that a fox should not be of the jury at a goose's trial – as per Dr Johnson – then, in the case cited by Lord Denning, *all* the jury should have been black.'

'Nonsense!' I said. 'Is it your inference that white jurors cannot be trusted to be impartial?'

'No,' said the boy. 'But Denning was certainly suggesting that black jurors can't be. Nor do his mathematics seem to be very good. In the case he cites, seven of the jury which acquitted the black defendants were white. Since you yourself insisted that white jurors are always impartial, it seems to follow that the defendants on this occasion were indeed innocent. Hoist with your own petard, I think.'

I played for time. I gave him hoist with my petard. I clipped him round the ear. Then a world-class refutation came to mind.

'If they were innocent,' I said, 'what were they doing in prison?'

'They weren't in prison,' said the boy.

I was only momentarily incommoded. 'I dare say they weren't,' I said. 'They will be soon enough, however.' (*See also* DENNING, LORD.)

Justice, British: The envy of the world.

The girl, Doreen, doesn't agree, of course, as she made abundantly clear when the papers in the matter of Alderman Entwistle, plaintiff, and myself of the other part were served by his West End representatives, Harbottle and Lewis.

'Did you know, Daddy,' she said, 'that for fourteen years after the European Commission of Human Rights was set up in Strasbourg in 1952, Britain denied its citizens the right of individual petition? Since 1966, when the Government finally conceded the right, more breaches of human rights have been established against Britain than against any other member state. In the last eighteen years, more files have been opened against the UK (eight hundred in 1990 alone) than against any other member state, and the same story is repeated at the European Court, where forty-three cases have been lost by European governments, of which seventeen have been against the British. I hope you'll put *that* in your TV programme, "Merrie England – Whither?" '

I encouraged her to continue for a while, since I had my refutation ready.

'Is that it?' I said.

I was glad I'd asked, since I now got an incomparably comic 'right-on' burst, which would have served as a leader in the so-called *Guardian*.

'No,' she said. 'The rights which have been upheld in these British cases have fundamental and far-reaching effects, like the recent ruling on the need for more control over telephone tapping and postal interceptions by the police.'

I suppressed a guffaw, refrained from pointing out that a man with nothing to hide would have no fear of his phone being tapped or his mail perused by the Old Bill.

'Other cases,' continued the girl, 'in which the British Government have been called to account include unjust restrictions upon prisoners' correspondence, ineffective judicial protection of detained mental patients, unfair discrimination against British wives of foreign husbands, inconsistent criminal sanctions against homosexuals, interference with the press's right to free expression, and inhuman treatment of suspected terrorists in Northern Ireland.'

Richly comic, eh? I was now ready with my refutation.

'If your instances are correct,' I said, 'which I don't suppose they are, they simply illustrate one of the most admirable characteristics of the British. Given the difficulties involved in getting a case heard in Strasbourg, the record says a lot for the tenacity and sense of outrage of British plaintiffs. Even if our authorities are the Europeans least concerned with human rights, we British can claim to be the most indomitable campaigners.'

Point made, I think.

Keeler, Christine: Do we have to be reminded yet again that Jack Profumo conducted afternoon liaisons with this international call-girl, deceived his wife, endangered the security of the State and lied to the House of Commons?

Surely not. He's paid his debt to society and should now be left in peace. I'd not rehearse the tired old facts again, were they not relevant to the matter of my peerage. The fact is, it appears to be a very English custom that sooner or later the eminent to the right of centre are caught up in an afternoon scandal with a foreign lass beneath their station. (*See* DE SANCHA, ANTONIA; LAMBTON, LORD; *and* MELLOR, DAVID.)

Is such a necessary condition of advancement? The furtive rendezvous with an 'actress', the necessary 'drop' at Victoria Station to forestall her kiss-and-tell memoir in the tabloid press? Exposure in any case, followed by the lady wife standing by one and smiling bravely at the garden gate, followed by two years in the political wilderness?

If such was the price of my advancement, I'd eschew it. The after-lunch liaison would be bad enough; worse would be Mrs Root standing by me, followed by two years doing charity work in the East End. I'd not want that, and have resolved accordingly to check with my friend Lord Chingford whether a liaison is of the essence. As far as we know, he's not had a rendezvous, and he's kicked up. (*See also* STATION, VICTORIA.)

Christine Keeler: The little international call-girl poses informally at home. Is she reflecting, perhaps, that the rewards of vice are having nothing to wear and only a kitchen chair to sit on?

Kipper, The Humble: An excellent subject for a maiden speech in the House of Lords. A lesson I'll remember when I myself am elevated.

Equally, the humble kipper has, traditionally, been an excellent peg on which to hang a comic column. This being so, I read to the boy and Mrs Root one day from *Cooee!*, by that most English of weekend humorists, Arthur Marshall, acquired off the remainder table at the Esher Fête.

'Mark this,' I said, 'by Arthur Marshall in the *Sunday Telegraph*. "Many people will recall, for it caused quite a stir at the time, a letter of protest written to a national daily a few years ago by a saddened Lord Olivier who, looking keenly forward to his customary gastronomic treat, had found himself travelling kipperless to Brighton on a train rightly famed for providing this appetising and fishy form of valuable, body-building protein. One wonders whether Lord O. was fobbed off with some lesser attraction. Were bacon and eggs suggested? Was the great actor coaxed to a plateful of watery scramble? History is silent on the point."

'Small wonder that Philip Howard, that most penetrating judge of English humour, once dubbed Marshall "Our Merry Nestor with a twinkle in his eye!"; still less surprising that Clive James – ever a generous arbiter of other people's work – has observed of Marshall's weekend essays that "This kind of thing is much harder than it looks." '

'For myself,' said the boy, 'I'm rolling in the aisles. Were you to read another such piece, I'd crack a rib.'

'In that case,' I said, 'you'll not be disappointed, since I shall shortly come to: "Amusing Place Names. Wagglewater." '

Lady Bountiful: The Lady Bountiful of old has, for the most part, been replaced by the so-called Social Services – the upshot, as the PM perceptively observed in an address to the Carlton Club, being a breakdown in moral values.

'Socialism must face the fact,' the PM said, 'that it is precisely where the State has intervened that local communities have been destroyed.'

That said, the concept of private charity still exists – to be seen as a rule among groups of privileged lunch-time ladies, who, having had their faces lifted once too often, have nothing better to do with their time than meet over a *veau escalope* and discuss the plight of those less fortunate than themselves.

As luck would have it, I recently attended one of these *escalope* get-togethers myself, albeit by mistake. Having gone to the Café Royal in Regent Street to attend a symposium of British Troubleshooters, at which Sir Jones was down to speak, I took a wrong turning and lunched instead with a group of hard-faced women with rings and hairstyles – 'Bubbles' Rothermere, was it? You'll know the sort – who were discussing a recent accident sustained by the Filipino servant of the lunch-time lady in the chair.

'Sir Root,' I said. 'Don't mind me – researching such as your-selves for Central Television. Budge up, madam. The *escalope* looks good.'

It would be a feather in the group's cap charity-wise, the head lunch-time lady said, were this unfortunate individual to be cured at their expense – or, rather, not at their expense.

'Tell me, Clarissa,' she said to the facial surgery victim sitting on her left, 'are you still in touch with that marvellous little New York surgeon? The one who fixed Jessemy's back as a favour to your husband?'

Lady Bountiful: Charity begins at the Café Royal. A group of Lady Bountifuls line up in Lord Forte's vestibule. £32,000 was raised for Baroness Thatcher's underclass (less expenses – gowns, pearls and so forth). They'll be celebrating tonight in Cardboard City.

Clarissa said she was – so the New York surgeon was in the bag and, more importantly, on the house – and then another lunch-time lady said that, since her husband owned an airline, the little Filipino could be flown to New York for nothing. At which point, a fourth lunch-time lady said that, since her husband owned a New York apartment block, he could be housed at no expense to the charity committee while waiting for his operation.

Once it was established that his back could be fixed for nothing, the ladies turned their attention to more pressing matters, such as cosmetic surgery and changed flight schedules. It would be easier than it was, it seemed, to get to Mustique. Then Clarissa produced her new electronic personal organiser and complained that she couldn't make head or tail of its instruction book. Nor, alas, could the others.

'It's the blind leading the blind here,' said Jessemy.

'I thought the blind lunch was next week,' said Clarissa.

At which point, the discussion turned – appropriately enough – to the honours system in general and the recent elevation of some obscure figure in the arts in particular.

'We all know how he got his,' said Clarissa. 'He's a friend of Dorothy.'

A useful piece of info. Dorothy must be very influential. I'd boast of my own friendship with her at every opportunity – and one such shortly arose. Wishing to excuse myself, I retired to the Gents, where I happened to find myself standing next to Sir Jones.

'Speech go well?' I said. 'Since we last met, I have become a friend of Dorothy.'

He was impressed by the info, backing out of the Gents in some confusion.

So – the spirit of Lady Bountiful survives in Merrie England. And of Lord Bountiful, I'm glad to say. My friend Sir Forte, the little caterer, had thrown the lunch in gratis. Plus, before departure, I was able to issue some invitations to my party on the 26th.

'An invite to my do, Lady Clarissa,' I said. 'Sir Root at home. Dancing in a marquee to a strict tempo dance ensemble. By all means bring your better half, if he's extant.'

A useful outing – more beneficial, in the event, than attending to Sir Jones addressing a symposium.

Lambton, Lord: Do we have to be reminded yet again that Lord Lambton conducted three-in-a-bed afternoon assignations – involving so-called 'pot' and bondage – with Norma Levy, the little international tart, and a lunch-time colleague of hers from Chelsea Cloisters (Big Brenda, was it?), that he deceived his lady wife (later affianced to Sir Worsthorne) and endangered the security of the state?

Surely not. There should be a privacy law, in my opinion, prohibiting such malicious repetition. I'd not rehearse the squalid details yet again were they not appertaining to the matter of my peerage and this apparent necessary condition of advancement: that at some point one is involved in a very English scandal.

As per my already described intentions, and in order to check this out, I presented myself one day at Lord Chingford's office in the Lords.

'Look here, Chingford,' I said. 'I'm of a mind, as you know, to join you in the Lords. Tell me this: is it of the essence that I'm first caught all ends up, as per our mutual friend, Lord Parkinson? Or, like Moynihan, the little Oxford cox, be seen waltzing at a Tory ball with a little Asiatic in research (so-called Pamella Bordes, was it?) Or wear a Chelsea football strip while arse up over a foreign "model's" knee, as per Mellor, the ex-Minister for Fun?

'You can speak from the shoulder. We're men of the world, you and I, we've knocked around a bit. You've kept your nose clean, as far as I know. Or have you just been lucky?'

'We're off the record?' Chingford said.

'Of course,' I said, activating my pocket tape recorder. This would be good. Chingford, it seemed, was about to make sordid inferences against himself – later to be repeated in a prime-time slot. He'd not be expecting that. He'd not expect, in a year's time, to settle down in his lounge-room after supper, only to hear himself confess on camera. I waited with bated breath and fully activated tape.

'In fact,' he said, 'I was lucky – in so far, at least, as I slipped through the net.'

'I see,' I said – scarcely able to contain my excitement. Imagine the delight of the fat man in Birmingham when I told him that I had Chingford making squalid inferences against himself on tape! Now I had to lead him on. 'What was it, then? They didn't twig? A *masseuse* in your basement, was it, as per Lamont, the little ex-Chancellor? An Oriental in research? Speak up, man. You're safe with me.'

'You misunderstand me, Root,' he said. 'It is indeed a necessary condition of elevation in the Tory Party that one should at some point be involved in a scandal. I'd always kept my nose clean, but for some reason an exception was made in my case. Perhaps they felt that I was too common.'

I strove to hide my disappointment. 'Surely not,' I said. 'You're no commoner than Lord Parkinson, when all's said and done – though he, perhaps, has made greater efforts to hide his disadvantaged background. Eschewing the drip-dry suits, unlike yourself, and cranking his accent up through one and a half sub-classes as per Lady Finchley.'

'You could be right, Root,' he said. 'However, that doesn't help you with your problem. Since a scandal is obligatory, what are you going to do about it? You haven't the stomach for an assignation?'

'It's not so much the act itself,' I said. 'No doubt the assignation could be simulated, later buffed up by Max Clifford, the little publicist, to the standard expected by the gutter press. In a nutshell, I could handle the *hors d'oeuvres*, as it were, but not the *entrée* and the *après-entrée*. I refer to Mrs Root sticking by me and the two years in the wilderness.'

Lord Chingford nodded sympathetically. 'I'm with you all the way,' he said. 'Like you, I always had a limited appetite for after-hours activity. Happily, I have the solution. There is a method by which you get the benefits of a scandal without the heartburn.

'All you have to do is instruct a shady character to leave a parcel of used banknotes on your behalf at Victoria Station. The media, tipped off by you, leap to the wrong conclusion and plaster defamations against yourself across the front page of every paper in the land. You trouser half a million for the slander, and you've been involved in a scandal without participation below the belt.'

'Chingford,' I said, 'I'm grateful to you. Here's an invite to my party on the 26th. Not a word about it to Lord Moynihan, the little cox. I'd not want him waltzing at my place with an Asiatic from research. See you in the Lords.'

At the first available opportunity, I'll be off to Victoria Station with the 'drop'. (*See also* MELLOR, DAVID; *and* STATION, VICTORIA.)

Language, The English: Here's one. Our most precious inheritance, as has been perceived by Booker of the *Telegraph*, along with the Monarchy, our sense of humour and the English sausage.

What can't be said in English can't be said at all, since it has at least five words for every concept. Plain obvious, you'd have thought, but ruminating thus one day (Booker had uncovered EC plans to 'harmonise' the languages of member States), I got into an argument with the boy.

'*Man ist was man isst*,' he said.

'Do what?' I said.

'The pun is untranslatable into English,' he said, 'which seems to refute your claim. Indeed, it seems to support the theory that existentialism is incomprehensible to the English precisely because of the ambiguity of the verb "to be": sometimes serving as a predicate – "I am", meaning "I exist" – and sometimes not, as in "I am fat and ignorant." '

I went on full alert, cocked the right hand, but held my fire. In the event, I was glad I had.

'The poverty of the English language,' he continued, 'is even better illustrated, perhaps, by the systematic ambiguity, and peculiar logical behaviour, of the word "good". Were you now to knock me cold with a clip round the ear, it would suggest that you were a good fist-fighter, but not that you were a good man. Small wonder that, because English is to become the official language of the Community, certain words are to be phased out, at the insistence of the *Académie Française*, either because they have disconcerting double meanings (Immanuel Kant is an example) or because they are offensive to our linguistically more fastidious neighbours. I refer to "pantyhose", "kinky", "wisecrack" and "nookie".'

'Is that it?' I said.

'Not quite,' he said. 'Asked why the majority of French, German and Spanish schoolchildren choose to take English as their second language, Monsieur Alain Laval, a professor at the Sorbonne, said, "I suppose they think that if the English can speak it, it can't be so very hard." '

I was lost for words. I caught him with a haymaker to the breadbasket. (*See also* LIFE, ELEVATING MEDIOCRITY INTO A WAY OF.)

Life, Elevating Mediocrity into a Way of: I waited for the boy to recover slightly, then asked him how he felt.

'A little better, thank you, Mr Root,' he said.

'In that case,' I said, 'listen to this by Lord Chalfont, the little arms correspondent in the *Sunday Telegraph*.

' "The most damaging effects," he writes, "of the elevation of mediocrity into a way of life are to be seen and heard in our language – at its best, as in the hands of masters such as Bernard Levin, Jeffrey Bernard and the late, lamented St Mugg himself – still the most flexible instrument on earth. Style and elegance in the written and spoken word are rejected as precious, affected and élitist. The BBC, once the model of grace and clarity upon which the standards of the civilised world were based, has been eroded by bands of illiterates who disfigure programmes with careless grammar, ungentlemanly syntax and the South Circular vowel sounds of the militantly uneducated." '

Then I hit him again, just in case. (*See also* LANGUAGE, THE ENGLISH.)

Line, The: The true Englishman knows that you have to draw the line, though he's not sure where. Some say it should be at 9 p.m., others at 10.

I'd opt for 10 p.m., arguing that such as myself who wish to monitor declining values on our TV screens – gratuitous bosoms and so forth from abroad – can wait till then. On the other hand, more elderly watchdogs, such as Mary Whitehouse and Richard Ingrams, argue that they have often dropped off by then, missing much that might otherwise incite them.

The debate continues, while we await a clear ruling from my friend Lord Mogg.

Liverpool: I've been reported to a hot line, if you please, and not by the boy *in re* the occasional clip round the ear, but by Doreen, the girl.

Here was the way of it. Over breakfast one day, Mrs Root took it upon herself – and with regard to *Root Around Britain* – to criticise my *modus operandi*.

'It seems to me,' she said, 'that we have entirely ignored the north of England. Shouldn't we visit Liverpool, for instance? It's ever so stimulating from all accounts.'

'So stimulating,' I said, 'that any Liverpudlian with two brain cells to rub together gets out of the place as quickly as he can. The Beatles, was it? They didn't stick around in the Tavern once "Yeah Yeah Yeah!" was number one. They were on the bus to London.'

'You mean the Cavern,' Doreen said.

'I know what I mean,' I said. 'Your average Liverpudlian's brain weighs half an ounce less than the standard obtaining in the rest of England and is obliged – since Belgians are similarly afflicted – to buy his hats in Brussels. Bill Shankley, having bought his flat cap locally, was unable once to give his half-time pep talk, since he'd not seen any of the game. He didn't make that mistake again. Mrs Shankley was seconded thereafter to shop in Brussels.'

The girl chipped in, of course. 'Bill Shankley wasn't a Liverpudlian,' she said. 'He was Scottish.'

Happily, I can think on my feet – even at breakfast-time. 'I am aware of that,' I said. 'Scotsmen, however, are similarly afflicted as to brain size.'

'We may be thankful,' said Doreen, 'that we're not discussing the size of sporrans. Heaven knows what racist slanders might ensue.'

Her point escaped me, so I continued with my dissertation.

'According to my friend Jimmy Tarbuck,' I said, 'and he himself comes from Liverpool, remember, the women are so ugly there that Liverpool is the only city in the United Kingdom in which nurses earn more than prostitutes.'

That's what did it. 'I shall report you to the neighbourhood hot-line,' Doreen said, 'for that vilely sexist slander.'

'I take my hat off to you,' I said. 'At least you've got more spirit than the boy.'

'I'm surprised you can find a hat to fit you,' she said.

She's a chip off the old block and no mistake.

London: In reality, London isn't a great city at all – although it is, of course – but a collection, as my friend Godfrey Smith has pointed out, of agreeable little villages – the down side being that the cheery citizens of one rarely venture forth into another. With Sir Branson's cheap flights, your average cockney feels more at home in Miami, the Balearics or Rhodesia than in Earl's Court or South Kensington. Nor is this surprising. As Godders has correctly observed, life *is* somehow more British in Rhodesia than in Earl's Court – with its local populace of hooded Muslims kneeling on prayer mats in the street and degrading the place with their unambitious hygienic systems – or South Kensington, with its ethnic teashops and mushrooming *patisseries*.

'We Londoners don't make use of our city,' Godders says. 'Before bowling down the M4 for an agreeable weekend in a country cottage, we should walk its streets, stand like old Wordsworth on Westminster Bridge and cry, "How fares the skyline in the modern world?" What does the average Londoner know of London's waterways? When did *you* last see our city by means of an historic walk?'

Mrs Root seems to agree with Godders. 'Are you, Henry, one of the many Londoners,' she said one day, 'who have never been, and long to go, on an historic walk?'

I hit that on the head. 'Certainly not,' I said. (*See also* SOHO.)

Man, The Small: I'm not yet fully accustomed to the girl Doreen's ruling that I must appear as 'the small man' in court when answering Entwistle's gagging order and other suits – assaults and so forth.

That said I agree one day to visit the Hackney Chambers of Shakespeare and Shakespeare, my representatives at law, in the company of Doreen and the boy. I've not led a particularly sheltered life, I think, but I take a step back, I can tell you, when I see their premises – a glass-fronted shop between an Indian take-away and a hardware store – and two steps back on being introduced to Mr Shakespeare and to his cousin, Mr Shakespeare.

'A word in your ear,' I say to Doreen *sotto voce*. 'They're black.'

The girl is quite unfussed. 'Of *course* they are,' she says. 'And a good thing too. Only they have the requisite street passion to represent the small man, such as yourself, who is a victim of injustice. I told you about the Highbury Two.'

I'm reassured, decide to put Shakespeare and Shakespeare at their ease by displaying the appropriate parlance.

'Twist and shout,' I say. 'Yeah yeah yeah.'

Shakespeare, or possibly it's Shakespeare – they're peas in a pod, I can't tell one from t'other – warms to me at once, says how confident he is that Entwistle's inferences will be dismissed when I appear before the Esher bench in three weeks' time.

'We're talking freedom of speech, Mr Root,' says Mr Shakespeare – or, equally, Mr Shakespeare – 'which is every Englishman's right, however small and humble.'

I bite on the bullet, resist an urge to flat hand my attorney in the chops.

'Right on,' I say. 'Yo. Safe, my man. I'll chill out until the 26th. Rock around the clock. Dig you later, alligator.'

I can hardly wait for the day of my trial. The Esher bench will not previously have been addressed by two dreadlocked Rastafarians with canary-yellow hats the size of pumpkins on their heads. I'm in good hands and, after we depart, I say as much to Doreen.

'First the Highbury Two,' I say, 'and now the Esher One. The Highbury Two were sprung, I take it? Their accusers banged up without hope of parole?'

'Oh no,' says the girl. 'They got six years each. They had to appear as small men, like you. How else could we have got them all that media coverage? And Shakespeare and Shakespeare received suspended sentences. It's quite unusual, I believe, for defence counsel to be sentenced too. "Mr Shakespeare," said the judge, "it's customary for officers of the court to consult their clients after an offence has been committed rather than before. Two years each, suspended." After that, their stock rose by a hundred and twenty per cent in this part of the world, of course. Shakespeare and Shakespeare know what they're doing.'

That's all right, then. (*See also* PORRIDGE.)

Marquee: I'm measuring the lawn the next day *in re* a marquee for my party on the 26th, when Alderman Entwistle (rtd) raises his head above the privet hedge and informs me that he won't be attending my do since he's planning a small 'at home' on the very same night.

I can't help chuckling at the man's audacity. Is there no end to the ignominies he wishes to inflict upon himself? Drubbed in court in the a.m., then, in the p.m., humiliated socially. I can see it now: Rolls Royces purring up my drive, disgorging *glitterati* from the capital.

'Evening, Sir Root. You're lucky with the weather. This is Lady Archer, my better half. Is that Sir Hambro dancing with your lady?'

'Sir Jones! How good of you to come! Mrs Root! Sir Jones here seems to be light of a vol-au-vent. Look lively, woman.'

Meanwhile a clump of disaffected local jacks-in-office and their suburban wives dip a fondue next door and peer enviously through the privet hedge. I can hardly wait.

'That's too bad,' I say. 'I was going to ask you if you'd cede your lawn as parking space. There'll be a Rolls or two from London, do you see?'

'That's odd,' says Entwistle. 'I was going to ask the same favour of you.'

The man's bluffing. He'll be lucky to draw the secretary of the

Esher Golf Club in a Ford Fiesta. (*See also* WEATHER, LUCKY WITH THE.)

Mellor, David: I'll not comment on David Mellor, our respected ex-Heritage Secretary, and the little foreign 'actress', so-called Antonia de Sancha. I'll not remind his blameless wife and children that he was entrapped in West Kensington in the early afternoon by an 'actress' in a *basque*. I'll leave that to the reptiles of the gutter press.

I will say this, however. I've engaged a local firm of bouncers to ejaculate any such as Miss de Sancha who may try to infiltrate my party on the 26th. I'll not want her sort cruising beneath the surface of my do. Nor types like Mellor, come to that. He'll be ejaculated too, should he try to use my party as a stepping-stone back to respectability.

Monarchy, The: Along with the English language, our sense of humour and the English sausage, the Monarchy is our most precious inheritance. It is the institution whose memories are our memories, whose big days are our big days. It is the very soul of the nation. The fulcrum of ceremonial. The source of our pageantry, which is the envy of the world.

Never, indeed, has it been more necessary to remind 'fun' republicans in the media – such as the New Brits of the Murdoch empire – that, in spite of the best efforts of such as Andrew Morton, the little investigative reporter from Australia, to some people the Royal Family are as real as the Archers. Further, that even such as my friend Major 'Ronnie' Ferguson and the Parker-Bowles woman have a role to play, albeit a comic one, in the Royal drama.

Major 'Ron', caught akimbo at the Wigmore Club, or the Bowles woman at the wrong end of a Squidgy tape, provide slapstick relief, as per Common and Ball in cabaret at Broadstairs or the rude mechanicals in a Shakespeare play.

Musing aloud, and along these lines, one day, I was interrupted by the boy.

'May I say something, Mr Root?' he said.

'Take the bull by the horns,' I said. 'The floor is yours.'

'For a start,' he said, 'Andrew Morton isn't Australian. He was born in Yorkshire.'

'I dare say he was,' I said. 'He certainly displays the defining chippiness and absence of *comme il faut*. Is that it?'

'Not quite,' he said. 'With regard to pageantry, it's worth remembering, perhaps, that at the Prince of Wales's marriage to Lady Diana Spencer the catering was masterminded by Monsieur Pierre Lacoste, a chef flown in from Paris for all such occasions since Churchill's funeral; the Director of Music was Herr Professor Otto Franck of Cologne University; the ceremonial troops were rehearsed in advanced drill techniques by visiting teams of Italian gym instructors; security was in the hands of Israeli commandoes; and Sir Alistair Burnet's televised commentary ("Even the trees are standing to attention in the Mall") was written for him by Mr Craig Brown, an Irish satirist, more usually employed as a restaurant and television critic by the Murdoch press.

The Monarchy: 'Pissing down as usual!' Our beloved Royal Family, in a customarily relaxed and informal mood, decide to eschew tea on the lawn and have their sandwiches instead in one of their many lounge-rooms. Truly it has been said that the family which takes tea together sticks together. An example to us all.

'Only the complex lavatory arrangements were organised by a British firm, which erected fifty portable toilets outside St Paul's Cathedral. At the end of the ceremony, the Dutch royal family left by a side door and walked into a septic tank.'

'I'm not surprised,' I said. 'They'd probably parked their bicycles in the wrong place.'

The boy hadn't finished yet. 'Your remarks,' he said, 'about Andrew Morton and the Murdoch Press lead me to suppose that you would consider the latter's decision to serialise the former's book – *Diana: Her True Story* – treasonable.'

'Certainly,' I said. 'Morton and my friend Andrew Neil of the *Sunday Times* were fortunate not to find themselves sitting on spikes at Traitor's Gate. What's your point?'

'Just this,' said the boy. 'Feeling as you do, isn't it inconsistent of you to continue dealing with the Murdoch Press? If I'm not mistaken, you took the Murdoch shilling yourself, furnishing them with an article about *Root Into Europe*.'

I was too quick for him, of course. 'A theory is not refuted,' I said, 'by the fact that those who believe it to be true fail to abide by its consequences. The statements "Andrew Neil is guilty of treason" and "I am happy to deal with Andrew Neil" do not in logic contradict one another.'

'Hoist with my own petard,' the boy said.

He's a good loser, I'll grant him that. (*See also* INTELLECTUALS, LEFT-WING.)

Money, Old: Money is either old or new, the difference being that the former doesn't exist as such, consisting rather in heirlooms, priceless commodes and so forth.

Those with new money – myself – my friends Sir Delfont, the little Russian impresario, Sir Trust House Forte, Sir Jones etc – have cash in hand or bits of easily negotiable plastic about their persons; can, on the spot, exchange one or the other for goods and services.

Those with old money, on the other hand (my friends the Duke of Marlborough and the Marquess of Bath) not having any, are obliged, when eating out, to barter with the restaurateur, paying for the meal by means of an antique commode – brought to the restaurant for just this purpose – or with the deeds to a small parcel of arable land with grazing goats.

The question is, which is more advantageous if, like myself, you're after an honour from the Tories?

If it's a matter of a quick 'drop' of unmarked banknotes at Party HQ ('Here's yours, Sir McAlpine'), new money is, obviously, of the essence. It seems unlikely that a knighthood would be handed out in exchange for a commode. One can't be sure, however, so I ruled one day that we'd put the matter to the test; seek to discover whether you're treated with more respect in a restaurant if you attend as old money in ancestral trousers, and pay for the meal with a family heirloom.

'Tonight,' I said to Mrs Root, 'we shall be dining at Esher's smartest restaurant – Los Dos Caballeros in the High Street – as Sir Root and Lady Root of no fixed income. Indeed, I shall pay for the meal with our oldest possession – which, if I'm not mistaken, is the musical cocktail cabinet shaped in the manner of a crouching Atlas holding the globe, given to us as an anniversary present by our friends Michael and Mary Parkinson. We must dress down – you'll be all right, but I'll purchase a tweed suit with mushrooms growing on it from the local Oxfam shop – and don't, whatever you do, mention my links with fish.'

The meal went well – the prawns *à la plancha* are the best in Esher, the mixed grill sufficed, and the cabaret (Juan and Rita, doing the flamenco on a table) so accomplished that I booked them to appear at my party on the 26th – but when I attempted to pay with the musical cocktail cabinet, the management demurred. Since, for research purposes, I'd left my money and all my credit cards at home, I was lucky not to find myself doing the washing-up. I seconded Mrs Root to do the washing-up, while I went home and thought the matter through.

You can forget old money, it seems – or rather the lack of it. To discover what the disadvantages of new money might be, I rang up my friend Lord Delfont, who very decently asked me to lunch at L'Ecu De France, his favourite Soho restaurant.

'Tell me this, Lord Delfont,' I said, once we were settled in over the *Sole Colbert*. 'Did the fact that you're common hold you back at all in the matter of a peerage? I refer to the fact that your friends tend for the most part to be equilibrists and Water Rats.'

'I don't think so,' Lord Delfont said.

'Just as I thought,' I said. 'Yet at the annual Royal Variety Performance, Her Majesty greets you affably, and sits through the show nailed to her seat by means of a surgical saddle. New money, you feel, has been no disadvantage?'

'None at all, I think,' Lord Delfont said.

'Good,' I said. 'In that case, you can pay for lunch. I represent old money, do you see? *Henri de la Rue of Harfleur.* My people came over with the Conqueror.'

Sir Delfont tapped himself about the upper trunk. 'I'm afraid that won't be possible,' he said. 'I never carry money on me.'

Later, as I did the washing-up, I rather regretted that, over an aperitif, I'd asked him to my party on the 26th. (*See also* WEATHER, LUCKY WITH THE.)

Moon: The true Englishman doesn't moon. (*See also* PRINCE ANDREW.)

Moore, Patrick: What an agreeable, and very English, irony that when the youthful Patrick Moore, hoping to become a cinema buff, went into the Eastbourne Public Library and asked for a book about the stars, they gave him, not Peter Noble's *The Great Years of Hollywood*, which he had wanted, but *The Young Observer's Guide to the Heavens*.

The cinema's loss was astrology's gain. With his panto haircut and distracted manner, Moore soon came to represent the acceptable face of science, a true Englishman, who pens comic operas in his spare time and is not afraid to offer his unfashionable views on law and order. (*See also* NORMAN, BARRY.)

Mortar, Bricks and: The boy Partridge seems to be learning. From time to time, he now shows an intelligent interest in his betters, asked me one day as we drove through Kent on an English summer afternoon, what was the secret of my success.

'Are we talking media standing now,' I said, 'the head in frame, a coffee-table book to follow? Or accumulated capital, residuals banked?'

'I'm talking accumulated capital,' he said.

'Bricks and mortar,' I said. 'In my day, bricks and mortar were an Englishman's best investment – a lesson I learned early in life. Shortly after I took over the family whelk stall from my grandfather, Henry "Cannonball" Root, at the business end of a writ, I was minding it one day when a toff in a Rolls drove up.

'I served him with two penn'orth of whelks, and then I asked him what was the secret of his success. How, I said, could I end up with a Rolls like his?

' "Work all the hours God gives," he said. "Save every penny and put the lot into bricks and mortar. In thirty years, you'll have everything that I've got." It was a lesson I never forgot.'

'You bought a house?' said the boy.

'No, I nicked his Rolls,' I said.

I wasn't stupid. Such of the working class as took Lady Finchley's advice and bought their council houses are the new poor, I gather. Saddled with negative equity and a patio fore and aft. You can't help laughing. (*See also* AREAS, NO-GO.)

Music: Judging music to be of the essence at my do on the 26th, I have contracted the matter out to the best people in the area – Party Planners Ltd of Esher High Street, who, in fact, can arrange not just music, but the whole shebang: tent, waiters, *vol-au-vents* and so forth.

'With regard to music,' I said to the lass in charge, 'versatility will be a requirement of the picked ensemble. There'll be a broad spectrum of society present, young and not-so-young, so I'll want everything from the two-step to the jitterbug, with an underthump of show tunes. Nothing too outmoded, mind you, and saving Lady Archer's presence. I'll not want a medley from *Annie Get Your Gun*, thank you very much. Nothing prior to *My Fair Lady*, should be the rule, with plenty by Sir Webber, the balloon-faced cellist. When it comes to the jitterbug, Lady Archer will have to sit it out.'

'I see,' said the lass. 'I suggest "Raving" George Dibley, Esher's best. He has a very wide collection.'

'A collection of what?' I said.

'Records,' she said.

'I dare say he has,' I said. 'But I don't want him bringing them over to my place.'

'So you don't want a discothèque?'

I could scarcely believe my ears. 'A *discothèque?*' I said. 'We're not talking about Caesar's Palace, Romford, here. I'm after a live ensemble.'

She got the picture eventually, suggested Arthur Lightwater and the Majestic Hotel Opheans.

'Are they versatile?' I said. 'Apart from alternating smoothly from waltz to hokey-cokey, they will be required to accompany the cabaret – Juan and Rita, flamenco dancers.'

The lass reassured me. 'Oh yes,' she said. 'When it's time for the cha-cha-cha or *pasa doble* Arthur becomes Arturo and the band put on black wigs, floral shirts and cummerbunds. I'm sure they could cope with the flamenco.'

That's all right, then. Arthur's been booked, much to the chagrin on the night, I imagine, of my neighbour and rival host, Alderman Entwistle. His guests will have to make do, no doubt, with Mrs Entwistle's wind-up gramophone and excerpts from *Cavalcade*. (*See also* WEATHER, LUCKY WITH THE.)

Nature's Gentlemen: Leaving the Hackney chambers of my new representatives at law, Shakespeare and Shakespeare, the next day, I happened to expatiate for Doreen and the boy on the subject of Nature's Gentlemen.

'Unlike Gentle Giants, with whom they shouldn't be confused,' I said, 'Nature's Gentlemen can be of any size – the defining characteristic being a grasp of etiquette in spite of a disadvantaged background . . .'

'I see,' said the boy. 'In that case, we can assume, can we, Mr Root, that you're not one of Nature's Gentlemen?'

I went on full alert. Was the boy inferring that I lacked a grasp of etiquette? As a pre-emptive shot across his bows, so to speak, I raised a hand, ready to clip him round the ear. Wisely, he reversed direction.

'I was merely suggesting,' he said, 'that you have too much background. *Baron Henri de la Rue of Harfleur* and so forth.'

'You're right,' I said. 'On top of which, I lack appropriate criminal connections. In this part of the world particularly, Nature's Gentlemen have, as often as not, got their feet a little muddy but are excused their misdemeanours because they love their mothers, are kind to children and give generously to charity. The Kray twins, who were not unknown to tip their close associates headfirst into a pile of wet cement, are recognised in these parts as Nature's Gentlemen.'

As luck would have it, I spotted at this moment one of Nature's Gentlemen across the road – a shabbily, but correctly attired senior whose careworn face suggested a hard life but an honest one, a brace, perhaps, of GBH convictions notwithstanding. I called the old chap over and handed him the Hasselblad, instructed him to take a likeness of myself, Doreen and the boy posed against Shakespeare and Shakespeare's chambers – a still of work in progress, as it were, for the fat one in Birmingham with the cheque book.

'Smile please,' he said, taking two steps back and then another one and then ten steps more, until he vanished round the corner, never to be seen again.

The boy laughed, I'm sorry to say. He'll laugh on the other side of his face when he discovers I've recovered the price of the Hasselblad from accumulated *per diems*. (*See also* GIANTS, GENTLE.)

Nelson, Admiral Horatio: Driving round Trafalgar Square later that week, I was struck by an oddity of English history.

'How strange,' I said, 'that England's two greatest captains – Wellington and Nelson – only met on one occasion and then failed to hit it off. Different sorts, do you see? Nelson, like Wolfe – the little victor at Quebec who bit his other generals – was a throwback to an earlier England, to the emotional Tudor England when men boasted and bragged and were unashamed to shed a tear. What have you got to say to that?'

'It's very interesting, Mr Root,' said the boy. 'Both, I believe, hailed from Tudor Cornwall, as opposed to Stuart Hampshire.'

Mrs Root rocked with laughter, I don't know why, so I continued with my dissertation.

'Further,' I said, 'it is interesting to remember that on two notable occasions both Wolfe and Nelson were thought by their contemporaries to have behaved in a manner unbefitting gentlemen. Before sailing to America, Wolfe dined with Pitt and Temple. After dinner, and excited by the thought of the great mission that lay ahead, he drew his sword and, to the embarrassment of his hosts, burst into a storm of *gasconade* and bravado, which shocked them profoundly. Shakespeare, Drake and Raleigh would have taken such behaviour in their stride.'

'You're very well informed, Henry,' said Mrs Root.

And so I should be. I was quoting from the picture-book which Mrs Root bought in the vestibule at Walmer Castle – the one which *Root Around Britain* will in due time subsume.

'Thank you, Mrs Root,' I said. 'One likes to know one's onions.'

'What's *gasconade*?' she said.

I played for time, puffed myself a little further. '*Root Around Britain*,' I said, 'will be recognised as the most authoritative work extant. I'll be . . .'

'Boasting,' said the boy.

I clipped him round the ear. 'You'll not accuse me of that,' I said.

Admiral Horatio Nelson: Here, the little upstart Admiral poses —
fully sighted — against a cannon. Like Lady Hamilton's better
half, and — in our own day — Baroness Finchley herself, he later
became famous for turning a blind eye to inconvenient facts.

'I wasn't,' he said. 'I was merely telling Mrs Root that *gasconade* means boasting.'

'We all know that,' I said. 'My point is that Nelson had precisely the same effect on Wellington on the only occasion they met. Wellington himself described the meeting thus: "He entered at once into conversation with me, if I can call it conversation, for it was almost all on his side and about himself, and in a style so vain and silly as to disgust me." No doubt the Duke would have been disgusted by others of an Elizabethan stripe, with their weeping and *gasconade.*'

'That's right,' said the boy. 'Nor would the Duke have approved of Nelson's incessant womanising.'

'Quite so,' I said. 'Wellington, as we know, pleasured Her Ladyship once in his top boots and once with them off. He didn't . . .'

'That was Marlborough,' said the boy.

I was astonished. 'I'm thunderstruck,' I said. 'Marlborough pleasured Lady Wellington in his top boots? Whatever next?'

'You misunderstand me,' said the boy. 'It was Marlborough who wrote in his diary the bit about his top boots.'

'I dare say it was,' I said. 'The point I was about to make, however, is that Wellington, as far as we know, only parked his boots under the wrong bed once. Lady Caroline Lamb, was it? The little poet's mistress? *Don Juan* and so forth? As essayed in the film of the same name by Sarah Miles? She's one. Vivien Leigh? She was another.'

'Oh, I did like Vivien Leigh,' said Mrs Root.

'No doubt you did, Mrs Root,' I said. 'My drift is, however, that Nelson hung his sou'wester here, there and everywhere, not least on Lady Hamilton's hook. As enacted by Vivien Leigh. That's my drift.'

'I did like Vivien Leigh,' said Mrs Root.

'Vivien Leigh,' I said, 'was no better than she should be. Led Sir Olivier quite a dance, I'm told. Danny Kaye, was it?'

'You're becoming confused, Henry,' said Mrs Root. 'I think you mean Peter Finch.'

'You astound me, Mrs Root,' I said. 'Peter Finch and Danny Kaye? It was as well for them the ladder and the long lens didn't obtain in their day.'

'No, no,' said Mrs Root. 'Danny Kaye and Lord Olivier.'

Kiss me, Hardy and so forth. Naval tradition, nothing more. I'd heard enough, however. 'Anything left of the pork pie, Mrs Root?' I said. (*See also* CINQUE PORTS, THE; *and* QUEBEC HOUSE.)

Norman, Barry: What an agreeable, and very English, irony that when the young Barry Norman went into the Cleethorpes Public Library and asked for a book on the stars, they gave him, not *The Young Observers' Guide to the Heavens*, which he had wanted, but a copy of Peter Noble's *The Great Years of Hollywood*.

Astrology's loss was the cinema's gain. In spite of his award-winning haircut and laconic wit – 'Cecil B. de Mille parted the Red Sea not once but twice. Even God couldn't do that!' – he quickly proved that an English buff will always prevail in a prime-time slot against a little *cinéphile*.

North-East, The Deprived: Mrs Root continues to witter on about the North, insisting that the fat man in Birmingham will want us to research north of Watford Gap, whatever that might be.

The Deprived North-East: Baroness Thatcher's Britain. These gnarled, self-pitying unemployed form a benefit queue, nostalgic, no doubt, for the days of 'trouble at t'mill'. The disused steel mill is now a heritage centre.

'I'm only concerned about the ratings, Henry,' she said one day. 'The good people of the Home Counties aren't the only ones with television sets, you know.'

She could have been right at that, but it seemed unlikely that such in the North as could afford consumer durables like television sets would be able to comprehend my message. As I've pointed out before, recent research shows that your bluff northerner customarily deploys just five hundred and seventy-six words of the language inherited from Shakespeare and Milton.

' "Awa' the lads!" is it, Mrs Root?' I said. 'They'll not understand a word I say. When Ossie Ardilles, the little Argentinian play-maker, became Newcastle's manager he was asked on local radio what his greatest difficulty had been in settling in. "The language barrier, John," he said. "The lads can't speak Spanish?" said the interviewer. "No," said Ardilles, "they can't speak English." A telling anecdote, I think you'll agree. Plus and further, who's the fat one with a knee?'

'Gazza, Henry?'

'That's the one. When Gazza joined the Italian club, Lazio, he told reporters that he would now be able to explete freely on the park since Italian referees wouldn't understand him. No one told him that Italian officials customarily speak excellent, indeed idiomatic English, and Gazza, to his surprise, received the yellow card for swearing seven times in his first six games – and as many corrections to his English syntax and pronunciation. What have you got to say to that?'

'If the Italian officials could understand Gazza,' she said, 'why couldn't Mr Ardilles understand the Newcastle lads?'

'You've got me there, Mrs Root,' I said. 'Be that as it may, I speak for Esher, not the deprived North-East. End of discussion, I think.' (*See also* LIVERPOOL.)

Omnibus, The Clapham: With two weeks to go still until my party on the 26th, the boy and I take a trip on the Clapham Omnibus – more accurately, the 137 trading between Sloane Square and Brixton – to discover what (as per Lord Devlin) the ordinary decent Londoner believes in his water to be true. By dint of quizzing on the top deck – 'Speak up, madam, we represent Central Television' – we learned that he believes, among other things, that:

It's all in the stars. If you're going to die, you're going to die.

UFOs are regularly sighted by the RAF, but this is hushed up by the Government.

Women are an alien species sent to earth millions of years ago by a malevolent judiciary on another planet.

The Royal Family lives in a goldfish bowl.

Gloria Hunniford is a very nice person.

Blacks are entirely lacking in body hair, which is why they can't swim. Throw a black into a pond and he'll sink like a stone.

By an ancient legislative anomoly, it is a capital offence to affix a first-class stamp upside down on an envelope.

Selina Scott is the fifth most intelligent person in the country.

Spinach turns your water green.

Lime juice is the most active depressant known to man, which is why German POWs were given gin and lime during the war to stop them wanting to escape.

Elvis Presley was spotted at the first night of *Aspects of Love* in New York.

Nuclear war wiped out the first race of intelligent human beings over two million years ago.

The Bermuda Triangle claims more victims a year than road accidents.

The Japanese live in apartments the size of matchboxes, sleeping on the floor to save space. Possessing a different body chemistry to Europeans, they turn as red as tomatoes and explode if they drink any alcoholic spirit.

There is a tribe living in the Andes who achieve an average age of a hundred and thirty-two. Their diet consists entirely of nuts.

Georges Simenon, author of more than three thousand books featuring the pipe-smoking Inspector Maigret, could complete a work in just three days, locking himself in a cork-lined room six feet by six and receiving his meals through a hatch. In his spare moments, he made love to more than six thousand local girls.

One sniff of cocaine and your nose drops off.

You can't trust a Frog or an Eyetie. On the other hand, Germans are honourable opponents who fight hard but fair – unless they've had a gin and lime.

A most interesting day's research, I think, and Devlin's faith in the ordinary, decent Londoner seems to have been amply vindicated. (*See also* DEVLIN, LORD.)

Party, The: My obligations to work in progress – *Root Around Britain* and its residuals – have not interfered in any way with preparations for my party on the 26th.

The tent, ensemble, cabaret and *vol-au-vents* are already on contract hire, a Major Domo has been engaged and invitations are in the post to personalities, celebrities, politicians and members of the chattering classes who might, I judge, if suitably 'encouraged', nominate myself *in re* a peerage.

Thus, appended to the invite, is a short PS as follows: 'Please find enclosed a small *doucement* for yourself, trusting that such will persuade you to bear my name in mind when the next round of gongs is in the offing.'

That said, I've not invited the fat man in Birmingham who holds the cheque book, since he's already in the bag. And such as are back numbers currently or a busted flush – Lord Weidenfeld of Nicolson; Sir English, the little ex-editor; Checkland of the BBC; Sir Mark, my neighbour; and the Parkinsons – have also been eschewed. It's for their own good really. I'd not want to embarrass them, any more than I'd want to embarrass my other guests.

Plus and further, some have been designated as what might be termed replacement guests – after the manner of an airline which might have seats to fill – and have been informed accordingly on an alternatively coloured invite card that they are merely on a stand-by call, possible substitutes, only, should socially more desirable folk drop out.

On this second list are: Sir Isaacs, the little opera buff; Cheetham, the opportunistic publisher of downmarket shopping fiction; the Marquess of Bath (in case the Duke of Marlborough is otherwise detained); my friend Major 'Ronnie' Ferguson; Lady Bollard of the *Sunday Express* and Mrs Root.

Their invite reads, 'This entry docket can only be redeemed at the door should an 'A' list guest drop out. Cold cuts will be served in the servants' quarters for 'B' list guests on hold.'

No one should take offence at that, I think. (*See also* WEATHER, LUCKY WITH THE.)

Porridge: Time was when the cheery cat burglar buckled down and did his porridge. 'It's a fair cop, guv,' he said. Now he demands his so-called 'rights' and riots on the roof. Worse, and thanks to liberal agitators in the media, there is little difference these days between a spell in Wandsworth and a week at the Ritz. In some top-security prisons, muggers, rapists and monsters in dog-collars are living so well they have had to install burglar alarms to protect their possessions.

Prince Andrew: The boy presents a problem. After an extended adolescence – spraying the media from a paint-gun, pulling faces from his Range Rover at street derelicts huddled over heat valves in Piccadilly, sowing his wild oats with those beneath him ('models', foreigners, George Best's rejects, girls called Koo and so forth) he settles down, marries an appropriate sort with shared interests – 'mooning' in Concord's executive cabin, throwing rolls etc – and is immediately cuckolded by a bald American. (*See also* ADVISERS, FINANCIAL.)

That said, York came up trumps during the great fire at Windsor Castle, formed a Royal link in the human chain and reassured the nation in its hour of anguish. For once, he eschewed the 'mooning' and the spray-gun and, instead, acted as the family spokesman *vis-à-vis* the media.

Perhaps the boy's come good at last, and, with Wales as mad as a meat-axe at the moment, has his eye on the succession. That would give the constitutionalists a headache. The bald American out, the Ferguson woman back in and on the throne, and her mother, the little Argentine polo player's widow, in line for the vacant role of Queen Mother.

Plus, and an even bigger headache for such as the little constitutionalist Lord St John Fawsley, where would it leave the common woman who recently spilt the beans on Major Ron? (*See also* MONARCHY, THE.)

Prince Andrew: 'Okay! Which one of you blighters is the Sugar Plum Fairy!' jokes the Prince of Patter. 'Takes one to know one!' ripostes Wayne Sleep, the little ballet virtuoso.

Publishing: Publishing, they say, is no longer an occupation for gentlemen. Time was when publishers prided themselves on being the servants of culture and education. Further, the great publishers of yesteryear had a *physical* love of books. Old Jamie Hamilton, they say, was once discovered in his stockroom actually *stroking* his books. You'd not see that today. You'd not see the little American from Penguin stroking his stock, nor the peculiar one from Pan. Now it's profit-hungry businessmen and skinny, power-crazed women in pursuit of shopping novels and TV tie-ins.

Nothing wrong with that. I'm a TV tie-in man myself. We must move with the times and so forth. With this in mind, and ever on the alert for old enterprises off the pace – such as could benefit from the services of 'Root and Sir Jones – Troubleshooters' – I dropped in one day on my publishers, Methuen, and wiped their backlist inadvertently.

I had to laugh. I'd driven to London, parked the car in the Fulham Road, introduced myself to the lass in the vestibule ('Don't mind me. Sir Root. Troubleshooter'), banged about in accounts and editorial, was surprised to discover that the former, far from being scratched out in a ledger by a crone with a quill, were entered into a computing system of a rudimentary nature.

'This won't do for a start,' I said. I punched the keyboard, was then informed by an operative that I'd wiped their backlist. 'No harm done,' I said. 'Babar the Elephant, Christopher Robin, Sue Townsend, the little anti-monarchist, was it? There'll be no great demand for them these days. A word with the greybeard in charge, if you'd be so good.'

At that point, we were joined by old Mr Strachan, a grizzled senior, who seemed quite exercised at the loss of his backlist.

'You can count yourself lucky,' I said, 'that it wasn't stuff in the pipeline down the drain – your autumn list, perhaps. I'm here merely to gear up your marketing procedures,' whereupon I punched the keyboard for a second time.

'Oh dear,' he said. 'That *is* my autumn list down the drain.'

'And a good thing too,' I said. 'Your successor can start with a clean slate. I'm ruling you redundant.'

So saying, I presented him with the model of Henry 'Cannonball' Root's first whelk stall, given to me on the occasion of my own redundancy. Waste not, want not. I know recycling. Then I gave him an invite to my party.

'No hard feelings,' I said. 'See you on the 26th.'

Quebec House: Driving through Kent on an English summer afternoon, I was able to abort a suggestion from Mrs Root that we stop off at Quebec House in Sevenoaks – the birthplace of James Wolfe, who, in the heat of battle, was accustomed to bite other generals in the field.

'That won't be necessary,' I said. 'Thanks to the brochure *in re* the Duke of Wellington, acquired by yourself in the vestibule at Walmer Castle, we know quite enough about Sir Wolfe to be going on with.'

And so we did. *Gasconade* and bravado, wasn't it? Sudden weeping and eating peas off his broadsword at dinner with Queen Anne. Which isn't to say that events at Quebec didn't point up a characteristic difference between the French *in extremis* and ourselves.

As every schoolboy knows, when Wolfe was felled at Quebec, his trumpet major, fearful that the rank and file might lose heart, propped his corpse upright on his horse – in the manner of El Cid, the little Spaniard – with the happy upshot that the common soldiery had at the French with renewed *gasconade*.

When, by contrast, Montcalm, the little French general, was killed, his men – as would have been anticipated by anyone who's seen the French play rugger – ran around like headless chickens. When Sella, the barrel-thighed French skipper, was kicked into the cheap seats at Twickenham in '91, the French team – unaccustomed to the English habit of getting their retaliation in first – went to pieces. Fights broke out in the three-quarter line, philosophical arguments in the scrum. So it was at Quebec. '*Sacrébleu! Mon général* no longer thinks, therefore he isn't! Let's have it away on our toes!' And the French infantry fled from the English muskets. (*See also* NELSON, ADMIRAL HORATIO.)

Queue-Barging: Among the finest of English inventions, the humble queue must not be overlooked – as I said to the boy one day as we lined up to catch the Clapham Omnibus.

'The queue,' I said, 'is one of our most valuable and democratic institutions. Even the Queen Mother, God bless her, has to take her place in the queue. Foreigners, attempting to board a London bus without first joining the queue, would do well to heed an episode in English History – of which we have never made much fuss – known as the massacre of the Scots in 1189.'

'I'm all ears, Mr Root,' the boy said.

Queue Barging: A line-up of stoical Londoners board the bus to Oxford Circus. Sir Winston Churchill famously sang the praises of the English queue, though he himself preferred a long ladder and a good safety net.

'Good,' I said. 'Here was the way of it. At the coronation of Richard Coeur de Lion at Westminster on 3rd September of that year, a number of Scots were killed by the crowd after they had pushed their way into the hall.

'The rumour quickly spread that the thirty-one-year-old King had ordered an attack on the Scots by way of celebrating his accession to the throne, and there were massacres in many parts of the country.

'It appears, however, that the original victims may have incurred the crowd's displeasure not because they were Scots but because they were queue-barging – and that the unacceptably large number of Scots slaughtered thereafter stemmed from a simple misunderstanding.'

'What a shameful episode,' said the boy.

Shameful? Had he, as usual, missed my gist? 'Nothing shameful about it,' I said. 'Scots, and other foreigners, would do well to remember that it is our very English desire for order, expressed in a willingness to queue for hours and an abhorrence for those who won't, which gives us and the Germans our close *rapport*. Ah – here's our bus. Look lively, lad, or that growling madwoman with a carrier bag will have the last seat.' (*See also* SCOTLAND.)

Raeburn, Anna: It's quite a conundrum, in my opinion, that while our agony aunts lead the world in the quality of their counselling, they are, more often than not, as crackers as their clients.

I happened one day to be perusing Mrs Root's copy of *The People*, which avers of its resident counsellor, Anna Raeburn, that 'She has honed common sense into a science' – citing as an example Ms Raeburn's advice to Size 32A of Birmingham, for whom the onset of bikini weather is an annual nightmare.

'Listen to this,' I said to the boy and Mrs Root. 'To Size 32A of Birmingham, Anna Raeburn writes, "Forget about your bust size, love. It's the person behind the tits" – you'll forgive the agony aunt's parlance, Mrs Root – "who does the living." Sensible advice, I think you'll agree, yet Ms Raeburn herself is, on her own insistence, a very damaged person; has, for the last fifty years or so been conducting a liaison with a casual lawyer employed by Mirror Group Newspapers.'

'Marjorie Proops,' said the boy.

'So do we all,' I said, 'but I fail to see what that's got to do with Anna Raeburn.'

As usual, the boy was off at a tangent.

Rantzen, Esther: She's another. Some regard her as the guardian of our civil liberties, while others point out that on screen you couldn't meet a nicer person. The debate continues.

Meanwhile, and with some misgivings, I have decided to invite her to my party on the 26th. She'll hardly raise the tone, of course, but I judge she might make a suitable nominating referee in the matter of my honour. Accordingly, I've enclosed a small *doucement* with the invite, asking her to fill in the relevant nominating forms on my behalf and pointing out my availability for such as *Hearts of Gold*. It would do my chance of a gong no harm, I judge, were I to be seen grinning next to Esther between a heart-swap tot, two pensioners on kidney machines and a pornographic carrot submitted by a member of the general public.

Esther Rantzen: The great campaigner for the small man in the street and his constant companion, the small woman in the street. A passionate upholder of civil liberties, not least her own. Here, Miss Rantzen smiles in triumph, having beaten *The People* all ends up in the matter of an uncalled-for libel.

Realism: Over breakfast one day, I drew Mrs Root's attention to the fact that there's a new spirit of realism abroad in the land.

'How do you know?' said Mrs Root. 'We've only been to Kent and Somerset.'

The woman's still trying to persuade me that our researches should take us north of Watford Gap.

'I can do the rest of England,' I said, 'from what I read in the *Daily Telegraph*. It says here that even in the deprived North-East the people are beginning to accept the harsh reality that we can't pay ourselves for goods we haven't produced. They're no longer complaining about social injustice and the right to work.'

'That's good,' said Mrs Root. 'They're optimistic, then?'

'No,' I said. 'They've given up completely. We'll not be visiting the deprived North-East. Pass the marmalade.'

Referee: The true English supporter likes to see the referee and touch-judges working harmoniously together – not least when benching an excitable Frenchman.

'Would it be true to say, Mr Root,' asked the boy one day, 'that you're the referee on this enterprise and I'm the touch-judge?'

'In a manner of speaking,' I said.

'That my opinion counts?'

'Of course.'

'In that case,' he said, 'I think you were wrong, during the recent England–Wales match at Twickenham to cheer every time an English prop gouged an opponent in the eye and to cry "Bench the little French daisy!" every time the latter sought to protect himself.'

'Who asked you?' I said. (*See also* QUEBEC HOUSE.)

Reverse: With regard to the honour about to be lobbed my way, I have recently discovered that, having been duly embaubled by Her Majesty, one is required – after a short exchange of sophisticated pleasantries – to leave the Presence in reverse.

Wishing to discharge this evolution with aplomb (one would not wish to go arse over KBE into the next chap up for a gong), I have accordingly been practising the reverse walk on my lawn – after the manner of bullfighters who customarily keep in trim, I'm told, by jogging backwards in their grounds with a sack of cement in either hand.

I was thus occupied the other day, when I went clean over a bucket of water thoughtlessly sited by the boy – he was washing the Jaguar at the time – and pitched head first into my ornamental goldfish pond.

'That's two *per diems* docked,' I said.

'But, Mr Root,' he said, 'I'm the touch-judge and . . .'

'Make that three,' I said.

Riot: 'The true Englishman,' I said to the boy one day, 'doesn't riot. Only ethnic minorities riot – as per Brixton, Toxteth and the Broadwater Farm estate.'

'But Mr Root,' he said, 'our island story is gloriously punctuated with riots. What about Wat Tyler and the Peasants' Revolt? To say nothing of the barons' rising against King John or Cromwell's Civil War.'

'Leaving aside,' I said, 'the difference between a riot and a revolt, all the instances you cite took place during history.'

The boy looked puzzled. 'History?' he said. 'One day we'll all be history.'

'Speak for yourself,' I said. 'Such as the peasants you mentioned were merely evolving; we've arrived. There's no cause to riot any more.'

The boy still hadn't had enough. 'What, then,' he said, 'of the Billingsgate Riot of 1989?'

What the hell was that? I played for time. 'The precise details refuse to come to mind,' I said. 'Jog my memory, if you'd be so good.'

'In the summer of that year,' he said, 'a group of enraged fishmongers staged a violent demonstration against EC tax concessions on haddock caught in French waters. Three revenue inspectors and a VAT collector were beaten to the ground by angry wet fish retailers wielding kipper fillets.'

'That's entirely different,' I said. 'An entrepreneur is entitled to wave a kipper fillet in defence of his livelihood.'

Ridley, Nicholas: 'A true Englishman,' as Lady Finchley rightly said at the time of Sir Ridley's sad demise. 'He was rude, arrogant, impatient with any but his own opinions and, at Eton, a notable flagellant with basted willow or rhino whip.'

To which I'd only add that he was a unique judge of what a true Englishman will put up with in his own back yard – not to mention slippery slopes, no-go areas and thin ends of wedges. (*See also* BASQUES.)

Scientists: The true Englishman takes what a scientist says with a pinch of salt – unless he's a TV boffin such as Patrick Moore, the comic astrologer. A scientist with a panto hairstyle in the service of light entertainment – that's all right.

As my friend Patten, the little educationalist, has recently observed, 'What is a scientist but a peeping Tom at the keyhole of eternity? More often than not, a scientist will tell us something we already knew, and there is a direct connection, surely, between the lamentable state of the world today and the gloomy fact that the number of scientists currently alive exceeds by several million the number of scientists who have lived since the dawn of time.'

A sobering thought. Plus, we should not forget the wise words of that other great Englishman, Malcolm Muggeridge.

'Science,' said Muggeridge, 'can explain nothing that really matters. A little science takes you away from religion, a lot brings you back again.'

To the true Englishman, science is 'Stinks'.

Scotland: Not content with her constant thrust *in re* the deprived, self-dramatising North, Mrs Root is trying to persuade me that the fat man in Birmingham will expect us to visit Scotland. I was forced eventually to bring some facts sharply to her attention.

'Argue me this, Mrs Root,' I said. 'Did Morton, the little Royal biographer, visit Scotland when researching his seminal book – albeit one about to be replaced by mine – *In Search of England*? Further, did Muggeridge and the other one do likewise when compiling their boastful collaboration, *In Johnson's Footsteps*? Of course not. None of them as far as I know, went higher than the Wash.

'What, after all, is Scotland known for other than the sporran,

Scotland: On Burns Night, a lone piper on a Balmoral battlement has set to music the Queen Mum's favourite of old Robbie's airs. 'It would fair put me in a passioon / To hae a wife whose coont was oot of fashoon.' I decided not to visit Scotland.

the bagpipes and the haggis? "Fair fa" your honest sonsie face/Great chieftain o' the puddin' race." Burns, was it? We'll not go to Scotland.'

'If you say so, Henry.'

'Thank you, Mrs Root,' I said. 'I've not finished yet, however. Even the Princess of Wales, I'm told – and she was a country girl at heart, accustomed to whistling winds and so forth – was unable to put up with Scotland. Balmoral, is it? The lone piper on the castle battlements? The great echoing rooms with their high ceilings and scything draughts? The little corpses of animals hanging from every wall? The dour, monosyllabic retainers all too easily mistaken for the headless ghosts of Robert the Bruce or James I? The gnarled ghillie sitting on a thistle and keening about his Highland past? Small wonder the poor girl fled to London at the first opportunity, for tea at Harvey Nichols with her friend Wayne Sleep, the little ballet virtuoso.

'We'll leave out Scotland, thank you very much.'

Scrum, Collapsing The: The true Englishman doesn't collapse the scrum. The scrum is invariably collapsed by a fat little Welsh prop – as was all too clear in this year's England–Wales encounter in the cauldron of bogus emotion that is Cardiff Arms Park.

The boy and I happened to watch this encounter on television and, to help him with a correct reading of the game, I expatiated every time the Welsh collapsed the scrum on an English put-in.

'Blow me, it's happened again!' I cried. 'Did you see that, boy? The English front row speared head first into the floor as if drilling for oil. The entire Welsh scrum should be benched.'

'If you ask me,' said the boy, 'it's Jeff Probyn, the English prop, who's taking the scrum down.'

I was thunderstruck. 'I'll not stand for inferences against an English prop,' I said. 'You're benched yourself, until after supper.'

'But Mr Root,' he said, 'you're the referee and I'm the touch-judge and I thought . . .'

'Never mind what you thought,' I said, and I clipped him round the ear.

'You shouldn't do that, Henry,' said Mrs Root. 'The referee shouldn't clip the touch-judge round the ear. It sets a bad example.'

'That's right,' said the boy. 'Shouldn't we, in any case, visit Wales? I'm sure the fat man in Birmingham will expect . . .'

'Don't you start,' I said. (*See also* WALES.)

Shakespeare and Shakespeare: A further meeting in chambers with Shakespeare and Shakespeare, my representatives at law. I have to bite hard on the bullet each time they refer to me as a small man – such designation being the nub of my case. Not that I have one, if Shakespeare and Shakespeare are to be believed.

'You must understand, Mr Root,' said Mr Shakespeare, or perhaps it was his cousin Mr Shakespeare, 'that you have no obvious defence to the various charges brought against you – least of all common assault and, since you ignored the injunction granted to Alderman Entwistle by the Esher magistrates, contempt of court.

'Our best chance is to present you as the small man up against the system, the victim of a bureaucratic élite organised to protect the interests of the ruling class. It is a scandal, of course, that this country has no Bill of Rights protecting the small man such as yourself, but in the absence of one there is little we can do other than throw ourselves at the mercy of the court.'

I was about to expostulate with the man, tell him that as a visitor to our shores it ill behoved him to pitch up in Merrie England, participate in our heritage – The Queen Mum, the British sausage, *Beadle's About*, the London Marathon, free teeth, kidney machines and so forth – and then to criticise our customs. However, a kick on the shins from Doreen caused me to bite on the bullet in the nick of time. I adopted a docile mien, confirmed that I'd be advised by him.

'Word up, my man,' I said. 'Yo. Safe. I'm in your hands.'

'Good show, old bean,' he said. 'I shall present you as the Esher One, a victim of injustice, a helpless little man. Are the posters ready, Doreen?'

'They're being printed now,' she said. ' "Free The Esher One!" under a picture of Daddy gagged and bound, and with his head thrust through the working parts of a guillotine.'

I didn't like the sound of that. 'Rather jumping the gun, aren't you?' I said.

'To gain maximum sympathy for the campaign,' Mr Shakespeare said, 'we must aim at a custodial sentence. It's almost impossible to get a campaign off the ground unless the victim is banged up for a decent stretch.'

That made sense. 'Right on,' I said. 'However, I'll not want to miss my party on the 26th.'

I twigged my mistake even as I spoke. If I knew Doreen, she'd now issue invites to the Shakespeares. I was right.

'Hasn't Daddy asked you?' she said. 'You *must* come, it's . . .'

It was my turn to kick her on the shins. 'A word in your ear,' I said, taking her to one side and speaking *sotto voce*. 'You can't ask the Shakespeares! You can't expect such as Lord Archer and Sir Jones to mingle socially with a brace of Rastafarians – excuse me, Mr Shakespeare – the latter having arrived on skateboards and relinquished their court attire in favour of canary-yellow hats. Where's your sense of etiquette and placement?'

'Don't be ridiculous,' she said. 'Anyway, you'll probably not be there yourself.'

That was true, of course. I'm in good hands. Thank heavens for British justice.

'Give me five,' I said. 'Twist and shout. Yeah yeah yeah. See you in court on the 26th.' (*See also* PORRIDGE; WANDSWORTH; *and* WEATHER, LUCKY WITH THE.)

Slopes, Slippery: No true Englishman likes to have a slippery slope in his own back yard. (*See also* RIDLEY, NICHOLAS.)

Soho: In spite of certain little local difficulties – likenesses of myself plastered all over Esher gagged and bound and with my head poised under a guillotine's blade – research on *Root Around Britain* continues at a pace.

Driving through the West End after my conference in chambers with Shakespeare and Shakespeare, we stopped in Soho, where I expatiated for the boy and Mrs Root.

'It will be interesting to discover,' I said, 'whether the old Soho – happy-go-lucky Italian cheese vendors; cheery cockney cat burglars; pub poets with carrots up their noses; the rude old tart who ran the Colony Room; punchy fist-fighters; Dan Farson relaxing in the gutter; Jeffrey Bernard vomiting over your shoes in the Coach and Horses – have been driven out by gay nude encounter parlours and topless sex emporia purveying explicit material from abroad. What the hell's this?'

Our way was blocked by the oddest sight I'd ever seen. A swarm of tiny Chinamen seemed to have lost their dignity, their inscrutability, their cleverness and, I wouldn't wonder, your laundry too.

Triads, Tongs, waiters, chefs had suspended their normal duties and were now dressed up as dragons. They waved rattles, set off cracker arsenals, displayed abnormal powers of balance, sat on poles, performed conjuring tricks with plates.

Soho: 'Yes, we have some bananas' carol these cheery Soho fruiterers (*above*). They've not been subsumed by mushrooming erotica, in spite of my friend Paul Raymond's tourist peep-show (*below*). We English have no need of nude encounter peep-shows. They're for visiting Japs and Swedes.

Small wonder that embarrassed Japanese tourists rolled their eyes and backed away.

'We've wandered inadvertently into the Chinese quarter,' said the boy.

'Have we really?' I said. 'I'd rather be trapped, I think, in a topless sex emporium. Follow me.'

We stepped rapidly towards Greek Street where, once again, I expatiated for the boy and Mrs Root.

'Once the most attractive of London's many little villages,' I said, 'Soho has been subsumed by rapacious property millionaires such as my friend Paul Raymond, the little hairdresser. The small shopkeeper has been driven out, I'm told, by mushrooming super-markets selling their homogenised wares.'

'That's handy,' said Mrs Root, 'I can do the whole week's shopping while we're here.'

I wish I'd kept my mouth shut. Happily, there were nothing but happy-go-lucky Italian cheese vendors, whistling their arias, tomato stalls run by cheery cockneys, French *viandistes* cheek by jowl with Spanish *pescaderias*. Not a supermarket in sight. We were out of the place in no time.

Sons, Problematic Elder: I may have missed a trick here *in re* the matter of my peerage. Musing over the difficulties my friends Marlborough and Bath have with their elder sons, it hadn't occurred to me till now that my own boy – Henry Jnr – might be an ace up my sleeve, as it were, *in re* my elevation to the peerage.

Since I haven't the kidney for a scandal as per Mellor, Parkinson or Lambton – the West Kensington assignation with a foreign 'model' or granite-faced lady from 'research' – it would be easier, I suddenly realised, to produce the boy like a rabbit from a hat, thereafter gaining sympathy from the attendant shame. To this end, I addressed Mrs Root one day.

'Where's the boy?' I said.

'I think he's in the drive, cleaning the Jaguar,' she said.

'Not *that* boy, woman!' I said. 'I'm referring to Henry Junior. I'm of a mind to get in touch with him.'

Mrs Root gave a little cry of happiness. 'Really?' she said. 'How *exciting*, Henry!'

'Never mind exciting, Mrs Root,' I said. 'Do you have his where-abouts? Is he at liberty, more or less?'

'He's in Amsterdam,' she said.

'Just as I feared. In feathers, is he? Dancing on a pedestal?'

'It's more exciting than that,' she said. 'He's now with a contemporary dance troupe – *Le Ballet des Hommes Nus.*'

I blanched, frankly, would have gone down had I not steadied myself against the musical cocktail cabinet. 'Good grief!' I cried. 'It's worse than I thought.' Then I pulled myself together, realised, in fact, that this was even better. I could produce the boy, have him arrested for appearing publicly in tights and then bask in the sympathy naturally accruing to his father. My friend Marlborough would eat his heart out. Blandford, as far as I knew, had not appeared publicly in tights.

'Do you have his address?' I said.

'I'm afraid not,' said Mrs Root. '*Le Ballet des Hommes Nus* move around a lot.'

'I'm not surprised,' I said. 'They'll keep one step ahead of the Vice Squad if they're wise.'

There was nothing for it but to put the matter in the hands of a private investigator, instructing one such to locate the boy and bring him back to Esher.

'The *Yellow Pages*, Mrs Root!' I cried. 'They'll track down anything, or so they claim, from books on fly-fishing to straw hats to wear at Lords. They'll list, unless I'm much mistaken, fat operatives trained to recover a boy. Ah! Here's one. Ron Trumper Associates. He'll do. Do you have a likeness of the boy? We'll not want the operative to pitch up here with someone else's.'

The woman searched through her handbag, shortly produced a photograph.

'What's this?' I said. 'The Sugar Plum Fairy, is it? Goats and monkeys, it's the boy!'

This time I did go down, taking the musical cocktail cabinet with me. I came round to find Mrs Root holding smelling salts underneath my nose.

'Never mind the smelling salts, Mrs Root,' I said. 'The likeness could work to my advantage. The media will not previously have seen anything like this. The photograph is worth a peerage in itself.'

I rang up Ron Trumper and Associates, made an appointment to meet covertly at Victoria Station, where I'd 'drop' the likeness of Henry Junior behind a rubbish bin – together with a monkey on account. If the media spotted the transaction, all the better. I'd be exposed by the Murdoch Press, later trousering half a million for the libel.

'Why Victoria Station, Henry?' asked Mrs Root.

'It's where these things are done,' I said. 'My friend, Lord Archer, the little airport novelist – he was one. You'll find that half the businessmen in suits, prowling Victoria Station in the rush hour, have got their feet a little muddy. I have Lord Chingford's word on it.' (*See also* STATION, VICTORIA.)

Station, Victoria: I pitch up at Victoria Station with the boy, point out the commuters with briefcases who have, all too obviously, got their feet a little muddy ('Bad luck, John. Catch you at it, did they?') Later, in the Gents, I find myself next to Lord Rawlinson, the distinguished Tory lawyer. I'm a little surprised, I must say.

'You in trouble too, Rawlinson?' I say 'Don't mind me. Lord Root. I'm a friend of Dorothy.'

He backs away, I don't know why. Then I leave the package which contains the likeness of Henry Junior and a monkey in used notes behind the nominated rubbish bin where, I'm glad to see, it is shortly recovered by Ron Trumper, my appointed operative.

I pose and loiter for a while, smiling furtively, for the benefit of members of the media who might be watching. All in all, a very satisfactory outing. With Henry Junior at home, appearing in Esher wearing tights and so forth, I'll shortly be subsumed under a wave of shame such as neither Marlborough nor Bath has ever known *in re* their boys. And, if Lord Chingford is to be believed, I'll pocket half a million for the slander.

Terpischore: *In re* my party on the 26th, and having discovered that it is customary, on such occasions, for the host to lead off with his lady in the opening waltz, I visit Madame Terpischore of Esher – 'Dance Classes, Old-Time & Disco' – to check on the price of an instruction course.

'Here's the size of it, Madame Terpischore,' I say. 'I'm at home on the 26th to London's glitterati in a tent, and when I take the floor with Mrs Root, I'll not want us, as a couple, to be wanting in rhythm and aplomb. What can you do in the time?'

'A certain amount,' she says, 'but we only have a week. I suggest we start right now.'

'We can't do that,' I say, 'the woman isn't here.'

'That doesn't matter,' says Madame Terpischore. 'I customarily take the woman's part, and will be able to improve your performance considerably by the 26th.'

She'd got the wrong end of the stick entirely. 'You misunderstand me, Madame Terpischore,' I say. 'I myself am adequately versed in all aspects of the dance, including quickstep and tango, and with a grasp of such as the Gay Gordons and the hokey-cokey. My enquiries centre round reservations I have concerning Mrs Root's lightness of foot and ease in the sudden variation.'

Madame Terpischore gets the picture eventually, and Mrs Root has duly been installed in a week's crash course – the cost affrayed by means of an invoice to the fat man in Birmingham under 'Entertainment – Tuition in the two-step *in re* Mrs Root.'

Trumper, Ron: Trumper, the private operative in charge of tracking down the boy, has run him to earth in Amsterdam. Accordingly, I have wired the price of their return by boat – no point in throwing funds around – having first alerted the frontier guards at Harwich to their imminent arrival and, anonymously, suggesting the full strip-search. The boy will be carrying substances, without a doubt, and his exposure as a drug-fiend, on top of his unmistakable appearance as an invert, will be the icing on the cake *in re* my peerage.

What a day the 26th will be! The boy locked up, my own triumphant stand before the Esher magistrates, and my party in the evening. I can hardly wait.

Wales: No one, I think, would dub me a difficult or intransigent man. I know when to make concessions, to put the wishes of others – however misguided – before my own. Hence, in a characteristically expansive moment, I have ceded gracefully to the boy and Mrs Root in the matter of a trip to Wales.

'All right, all right,' I said. 'I'll not visit Scotland but, if it means so much to you both, we'll make a brief sortie across the border into Wales after my two triumphs – social and legislative – on the 26th.'

'Oh hooray!' cried Mrs Root.

'If I were you, Mrs Root,' I said, 'I'd save my "hoorays" until after our safe return to Esher.'

I then gave them a brief cautionary resumé of what we might come up against in this dark, primitive and neurotic land. When not muttering at street corners, dancing in circles, reciting self-pitying dirges and flagellating themselves with leeks, the Welsh, I said, dress up as druids and inflict religious incisions on one another with golden sickles.

'Never mind a welcome in the valleys, Mrs Root,' I said, 'you'll be lucky not to be hung up in a wickerwork container and immolated as a witch.'

The excellent mood I was in had been caused, I think, by news from my operative in Amsterdam. He'd persuaded the boy, by means of a 'sweetener', to return with him to England. The frontier guards have been alerted to the fact that two dangerous drug-fiends – one a transvestite, the other not – will shortly attempt to gain entry to our shores. My nominated honour's in the bag.

Wales: Having done the weekly shop-up in Swansea High Street, a group of typical Welshmen and their wives meet to discuss so-called EC subsidies. They're due for a rebate, they think, *in re* the leek mountain.

Wally: Party Planners Ltd of Esher have come up trumps – proving themselves to be not only providers of tents, *vol-au-vents* and live ensembles, but experts in social security too, by which I mean, not scroungers off the State, but large men in suits a size too small, who will, for a wage, ejaculate such as you deem undesirable from a do or function.

This morning, and by their instruction, an ex-professional boxer on their books – forty-seven fights, six convictions – named Mr Wally Peterson pitched up at my place for an interview.

I gave him a list of those who, if they tried to infiltrate, should be expelled – young Blandford; Lord Weidenfeld of Nicolson; Sir Issacs, the little opera buff; Cheetham, the supremo of the shopping novel; the Rantzen woman if accompanied by Desmond; and then, on a sudden inspiration, I took him across the privet hedge, where we rang on Alderman Entwistle's door.

The latter blanched, frankly, when he saw us standing there. 'I hope for your sake, Mr Root,' he said, 'that you'll not try intimidation for a second time.'

'Relax, Entwistle,' I said. 'I'm here to do you a favour *in re* your ill-considered do on the 26th. Mr Peterson here has been hired by myself to eject from my own do on that date "B" list glitterati who may try to crash my tent. It occurs to me that you yourself will be short of glitterati and might be grateful for my overflow. With that in mind, I suggest that Mr Peterson acts as a tosser-out at my place and a tosser-in at yours, lobbing over the privet hedge such as fail to measure up on my side, but would raise the tone substantially on yours. I refer to such as Lord Weidenfeld of Nicolson and the Raeburn woman. I'll not want the Raeburn woman counselling my other guests on PMT while they're trying to down a *vol-au-vent.*'

The fool, Entwistle, tried to bluff it out. 'I assure you,' he said, 'that my own guest list is perfectly satisfactory.'

'Really?' I said. 'You've drawn the Secretary of the Golf Club, have you? The branch manager of the local Asda store and his common wife? I'm impressed in spite of myself. That said, should Lord Weidenfeld or the Raeburn woman come head first through the privet hedge on the wrong end of Mr Peterson's boot you'll know what's going on.'

Poor man. Humiliated in court in the early a.m., confounded socially in the evening. I can hardly wait to see his face. He'll be the laughing stock of Esher.

Wandsworth: The big day dawns. My court case in the morning, my party in the evening. I'm up early, dress in legislative attire – sober suit by Peter Jones, Old Harrovian tie acquired for occasions such as this – and set forth for the Magistrates Court.

Mrs Root wishes to lend moral support, but I explain that I'll not need that. It's Entwistle who'll need moral support, I say, and it's better that Mrs Root should stay at home, overseeing the final arrangements for my party in the evening – the tent erected, the music podium in place, the *vol-au-vents* ready in the pantry – and practising the waltz and quickstep. I'll not want to be confounded by her lack of ease in the sudden twirl or variation.

Arrived at court, a brief word with Shakespeare and Shakespeare, my representatives at law, who have eschewed, I note, canary-yellow Rasta hats in favour of sober suits like mine. Mr Shakespeare, or possibly it's Mr Shakespeare – I still can't tell one from t'other (a problem I'll wager my opponent doesn't have with his people, Harbottle and Lewis of the other part) – momentarily discommodes me by saying he hopes I have with me a clean shirt, toothbrush and shaving kit.

'If all goes well,' he says, 'you'll be going straight from court in a Black Maria. First stop Wandsworth.'

I put this down as a 'right-on' joke of some sort, chuckle briefly and take my place in the dock.

'How do you plead?' asks Brigadier Dalrymple-Downes, the Chairman of the bench, its other members being old Lady Fortescue and Fred Appleby, a local tradesman whom I once flat-handed as an extortioner in Esher High Street.

Before I can answer, Shakespeare, or Shakespeare, is on his feet. 'Guilty, your honour!' he cries.

'I'm not referring to you, Mr Shakespeare,' says Brigadier Dalrymple-Downes. 'I was addressing your client, Mr Root.'

'Guilty!' cries Mr Shakespeare.

'Right on!' shouts Doreen from the public gallery, earning a rebuke from Brigadier Dalrymple-Downs. Another such ejaculation, he infers, and Doreen will join me in the dock.

I tug at Mr Shakespeare's sleeve, enquire as to how our case is shaping up.

'Excellently, Mr Root,' he says. 'I've got this lot over a barrel here. My speech in mitigation will swing the court my way.'

And so it does. Mr Shakespeare, on my behalf, now compares the current proceedings to a kangaroo court in the Third Reich. Brigadier Dalrymple-Downes is measured, rather to his disadvantage, against

Adolf Hitler. Lady Fortescue is dubbed a lickspittle, Fred Appleby a Nazi running-dog. The law is a right-wing conspiracy, he says, set up to prevent such as his client, Mr Root, from identifying Alderman Entwistle as the Tory gangster that he is.

'Fascist pigs, the lot of you!' he cries.

'Right on!' shouts Doreen from the public gallery.

We're doing well, I think, and then Brigadier Dalrymple-Downes – after a brief word with Lady Fortescue and Fred Appleby – hands his verdict down. It's six months for me for various contempts – alas, he says, the longest sentence at his immediate disposal – and six months for Mr Shakespeare for his performance here.

I clamber unsteadily to my feet, intend to say a word or two in my defence, but am interrupted by a sudden hubbub at the back of the court. Henry Junior, who has arrived suddenly from out of the blue with Mrs Root, seeks leave to speak. My heart sinks. I prepare myself to hear my sentence doubled.

'And who are you?' asks Brigadier Dalrymple-Downes.

'Henry Root Junior,' says the boy. 'My father's son.' And then he's off. 'I beg leniency,' he says, 'for the simple man you see before you in the dock. An ignorant fishmonger from the East End of London, he lacked the advantages which you and I, your Honour, could always take for granted.' I groan. The boy's exacting a terrible revenge. He's come to bury me forever – and after all I've done for him! 'My father,' the boy continues, 'recognised one obligation only: that he must toil night and day, up to his elbows in wet fish, to provide for his wife and children. And provide he always did. All right, he's rough and ignorant, lacking the acquired wisdom and ease of address which you, your Honour, have so abundantly displayed today. Is he now to be punished for this lack of sophistication? Because of his selfless support, I stand before you as the lead dancer with *Le Ballet des Hommes Nus* . . .'

My head sinks into my chest. That's done it, I think, but at this point Fred Appleby intervenes.

'*Le Ballet des Hommes Nus*, did you say?'

'Indeed, your Honour,' says the boy.

'One of my favourite companies,' says Appleby. 'I congratulate you. Your troupe has immeasurably enlarged the vocabulary of modern dance.'

'Thank you, your Honour,' says the boy. 'Tonight we are booked to perform in front of the Dutch royal family, but I have informed their Majesties that I shall be in no mood to dance, knowing that my father is languishing in prison. He is a simple man, but a good one –

and I love him dearly. I'm grateful to you, your Honour, for hearing me out. I thank you.'

The boy sits down. I'm dead meat now. They can put me in Wandsworth and throw away the key. Then, to my amazement, the Brigadier announces that, in all his years on the bench, he's never heard such a moving speech in mitigation. Further, that, with his colleagues' approval, he is now of a mind to change the verdict, releasing me into the loving care of the boy.

'Would that be acceptable, Mr Root Junior?' he says.

'Your Honour,' says the boy, 'nothing would make me happier.'

Lady Fortescue wipes away a tear, Mrs Root is similarly over-come, and Henry Junior tries his damndest to embrace me. I clutch at him briefly – in case the media are here – then manage to disengage myself.

'I love you so much, Daddy,' he says.

'Well – er – yes, I dare say you . . . You'll not be staying, I take it?'

'Alas, no,' he says. 'I'll have to catch the next plane back to Amsterdam. Curtain up at 8.30. The show must go on, you know!'

'Thank God for that,' I say.

Weather, Lucky with the: That, then, had been a narrow squeak. Happily, and thanks to the way I'd conducted myself in court, I'm able to line up with Mrs Root at 8 p.m., ready to greet our guests.

'We're lucky with the weather, Mrs Root,' I say. 'You didn't bother to change, then?'

'Oh Henry!' she cries. 'Whatever do you mean? This is the dress I wore on our honeymoon. Don't you remember? We danced all night and you said I was . . .'

'Don't start,' I say.

I check the *vol-au-vents*, issue the hired waiters with their orders, ascertain that security, in the shape of Mr Wally Peterson, is fully furnished with a list of undesirables, instruct Arthur Lightwater and the Majestic Hotel Ensemble to lead off with 'I Could Have Danced All Night'. 'And slow the tempo down,' I say, 'should Lady Archer take the floor. We'll not want accidents.' Then the boy arrives with Doreen, the latter having decided, it seems, to pitch up as she is – building-site boots and a teeshirt with a political message on its front.

'Oh dear, you've been in a fight,' I say.

'I'm not staying,' she says. 'I'm off to a street party in aid of the Hackney Two.'

'That's good,' I say. 'And who might they be?'

'Your exploited attorneys-at-law,' she says. 'Right now they're banged up in Wandsworth as political victims of injustice. Great, eh? It promises to be the best campaign ever.'

'Well, I mustn't keep you,' I say.

Doreen looks round the tent. 'No one's arrived,' she says.

'It's early yet,' I say.

What a night this is going to be! I blow out my chest, stretch the thighs, accompany myself in a small two-step round the floor, pause in mid-variation when I hear the sounds of music and laughter issuing from Alderman's house next door. Poor man! What a sorry affair his do will be compared to mine. I'm half inclined to pop across the privet hedge and snigger at his turnout, then decide that to do so would be beneath me. Instead, I speculate as to which of my guests will pitch up first, deciding to put my money on Sir Jones. Sir Jones famously likes to get his money's worth – will want first go at the *vol-au-vents* before inroads are made by others.

I rehearse my mode of welcome. 'Ah – Sir Jones! Glad you could make it! Help yourself to a *vol-au-vent*. Lord Rawlinson! How good of you to come! Sort out that little difficulty at Victoria Station, did you? Your secret's safe with me. Goats and monkeys, it's the Rantzen woman! Into the pantry, if you'd be so good. You're on hold.'

'It's half-past nine,' says Mrs Root, 'and no one's come.'

'The night is young,' I say. 'It's customary for the *glitterati* to pitch up late.'

At half-past ten I get a feeling of slight unease, instruct Partridge to check on Entwistle's do next door. He returns in minutes.

'I've found your guests, Mr Root,' he says.

'What a relief!' I cry. 'Just coming up the drive, are they?'

'No,' he says. 'They seem to have been drawn into Mr Entwistle's party. All of them, I'm afraid – Lord and Lady Archer, Lord Rawlinson, Sir Worsthorne, Lord Tebbit, Nigel Dempster, Lord Gowrie, the Duke of Marlborough, even the Raeburn woman.'

'He's welcome,' I say, 'to the Raeburn woman.' In fact, I feel a trifle faint. 'You pointed out their mistake, did you? They're on their way here now?'

'I'm afraid not,' says Partridge. 'They prefer the music there, they say. Mr Entwistle turns out to have booked "Raving" George Dibley and his travelling discothèque.'

I give it another hour, then lose my rag. I'll not have this. I'll not be socially upended by a local jack-in-office. I instruct my bouncer, Wally Peterson, to cross the privet hedge and 'persuade' my guests back here. The last person 'unpersuaded' by Mr Peterson ended up in a municipal rubbish tip, I'm told.

'I've not done that before,' says Mr Peterson. 'As a rule I throw people out, not in.'

'There's a first time for everything,' I say.

He disappears, is later to be seen across the privet hedge dancing with my guests – now, more accurately, perhaps, Entwistle's guests – thereafter chatting with Lord Weidenfeld of Nicolson, who, no doubt, is trying to secure a commission on his memoirs. Entwistle's party has turned out to be a social Bermuda Triangle, sucking in whosoever comes within its orbit.

Arthur Lightwater and the Majestic Hotel Ensemble play on. I accompany Mrs Root in the last dance. 'The party's over . . . it's time to pack up and go . . .' Music and laughter drift our way across the privet hedge.

We turn out the lights and make our way upstairs.

'Look on the bright side, Henry,' says Mrs Root. 'We'll not be short of *vol-au-vents*.'

'Nor we will, Muriel,' I say. 'And we were lucky with the weather.'